The ChatGPT Handbook for Beginners

Automate Tasks and Boost Your Productivity With AI— Quick and Easy

Jakob Huber

© **Copyright 2025 - All rights reserved.**

The content contained within this book may not be reproduced, duplicated or transmitted without direct written permission from the author or the publisher.

Under no circumstances will any blame or legal responsibility be held against the publisher, or author, for any damages, reparation, or monetary loss due to the information contained within this book, either directly or indirectly.

Legal Notice:

This book is copyright protected. It is only for personal use. You cannot amend, distribute, sell, use, quote or paraphrase any part, or the content within this book, without the consent of the author or publisher.

Disclaimer Notice:

Please note the information contained within this document is for educational and entertainment purposes only. All effort has been executed to present accurate, up to date, reliable, complete information. No warranties of any kind are declared or implied. Readers acknowledge that the author is not engaged in the rendering of legal, financial, medical or professional advice. The content within this book has been derived from various sources. Please consult a licensed professional before attempting any techniques outlined in this book.

By reading this document, the reader agrees that under no circumstances is the author responsible for any losses, direct or indirect, that are incurred as a result of the use of the information contained within this document, including, but not limited to, errors, omissions, or inaccuracies.

Table of Contents

INTRODUCTION 1

CHAPTER 1: WHAT IS CHATGPT? 4

    WHAT CHATGPT CAN DO 5
    THE ORIGINS OF CHATGPT 8
    HOW DOES CHATGPT WORK? 9
    MISCONCEPTIONS ABOUT CHATGPT 10

CHAPTER 2: GETTING STARTED WITH CHATGPT 13

    SETTING UP YOUR CHATGPT ACCOUNT 13
    NAVIGATING THE CHATGPT INTERFACE 17
    CHOOSING THE RIGHT CHATGPT SUBSCRIPTION MODEL 26

CHAPTER 3: MASTERING PROMPT ENGINEERING 28

    WHAT IS PROMPT ENGINEERING? 28
    GUIDELINES FOR CRAFTING EFFECTIVE PROMPTS 29
    USING THE SECRET PROMPT FORMULA 30
    TIPS FOR EFFECTIVE PROMPTING 36

CHAPTER 4: PRACTICAL APPLICATIONS OF CHATGPT 41

    WRITING 42
    SOCIAL MEDIA CONTENT CREATION 44
    BRAINSTORMING AND IDEA GENERATION 44
    LEARNING AND TUTORING SUPPORT 46
    PRODUCTIVITY TOOLS AND ADVICE 47
    CODING ASSISTANCE 50
    DIVERSE APPLICATIONS 51

CHAPTER 5: SEARCHING THE WEB 53

    WHAT IS SEARCHING THE WEB? 53
    HOW TO USE THE WEB SEARCH FEATURE 55
    CRAFTING EFFECTIVE WEB SEARCH PROMPTS 55
    LIMITATIONS AND CONSIDERATIONS 56

CHAPTER 6: ATTACHING FILES TO YOUR PROMPT 58

HOW TO USE THE ATTACH FILE FEATURE 58
APPLICATIONS AND USE CASES 59

CHAPTER 7: CREATING IMAGES 65

GENERATING IMAGES WITH CHATGPT 65
HOW TO GENERATE IMAGES USING CHATGPT 66
APPLICATIONS AND USE CASES 68
THE SECRET PROMPT FORMULA FOR EFFECTIVE IMAGE GENERATION 70
IMAGE PROMPTING STRATEGIES 84
REFINING AND ADJUSTING IMAGES 86
USING GEN-ID FOR VISUAL CONSISTENCY 91
TIPS AND LIMITATIONS FOR IMAGE GENERATION 93

CHAPTER 8: VOICE MODE 98

ACTIVATING VOICE MODE 98
USING VOICE MODE AS A LIVE TRANSLATOR 99

CHAPTER 9: THE CHATGPT APP 101

GETTING STARTED WITH THE CHATGPT APP 101
EXCLUSIVE FEATURES OF THE MOBILE APP 102

CHAPTER 10: PERSONALIZING CHATGPT 105

CUSTOM INSTRUCTIONS 105
MEMORY 109
KEY DIFFERENCES BETWEEN CUSTOM INSTRUCTIONS AND MEMORY 112

CHAPTER 11: CUSTOM GPTS AND GPT STORE 114

WHAT ARE CUSTOM GPTS? 114
EXPLORING THE GPT STORE 115
EXAMPLES OF CUSTOM GPTS AND THEIR APPLICATIONS 117

CHAPTER 12: CHATGPT LIMITATIONS AND ERRORS 119

CORE LIMITATIONS OF CHATGPT 119
COMMON TYPES OF TECHNICAL ERRORS 122
BEST PRACTICES FOR SEAMLESS INTERACTION 124

CONCLUSION 126

YOUR NEXT STEPS 126
OUTLOOK ON THE FUTURE 127

REFERENCES **128**

YOUR READY-TO-USE PROMPT FORMULA REFERENCE GUIDE **132**
    THE SECRET PROMPT FORMULA 133
    THE SECRET PROMPT FORMULA FOR EFFECTIVE IMAGE GENERATION 144

Introduction

What if you had a tool that could simplify your work and spark creativity while saving you hours every week to focus on other engagements you like? ChatGPT offers a chance to revolutionize how you approach tasks, projects, and even everyday challenges, but figuring out how to use it effectively can feel overwhelming.

Maybe you've heard about ChatGPT but aren't sure how it can help you and where to start. Perhaps you've tried it and felt stuck, unsure how to phrase prompts to get meaningful results. Alternatively, you might already be using it, but sense that there's more potential waiting to be unlocked—new applications, additional features, more effective strategies, better ways to streamline tasks, and boost productivity.

If that sounds like you, you're not alone. Whatever brought you here, this book is designed to address most of your concerns about using ChatGPT. Whether you're an author, marketer, freelancer, student, or someone looking to work smarter, this guide will show you how to harness ChatGPT and unlock its full potential. How do I know this? Because I've been exactly where you are.

I still remember the day I was sitting in a café in Lisbon, sipping coffee with a friend. He leaned over and said, "Hey, check this out." He opened his laptop, pulled up ChatGPT, and asked it to create a personalized fitness plan. Within seconds, the response appeared—detailed and actionable. I was astonished. How could it be so intuitive and powerful? From that moment, I was hooked and began experimenting, using ChatGPT for everything from summarizing books to drafting emails and brainstorming creative ideas. Along the way, I learned through trial and error while experimenting with prompts as I uncovered new possibilities and tested their limits. After a journey of discovery, ChatGPT became my assistant, tutor, and creative partner.

But it wasn't all smooth sailing. Initially, I struggled to phrase my queries right, and the responses weren't reflecting my ideas. Over time, I found strategies and techniques that made all the difference. In the beginning, I also wasn't sure when or for which tasks ChatGPT could assist me, but through extensive experimentation, I discovered a wide range of use cases where it's incredibly helpful. Looking back, I realized how much I would've appreciated having a concise resource to fast-track my learning—something that distilled the most valuable lessons into an easy-to-follow guide. That's why I wrote this book: to spare you the trial-and-error process and help you become a confident ChatGPT user faster and easier. Together, we'll explore how to make ChatGPT work for you, regardless of your experience level or goals.

If you have tried similar resources before, you may worry about whether you will get value for your time. This book strikes the perfect balance between theory and hands-on exercises. While other books may overwhelm you with dry, theoretical knowledge, this guide is designed to be practical, user-friendly, and focused on real-world applications. Unlike dense, complicated manuals, it simplifies the complexities of AI into clear, actionable steps that are easy to understand and fast to apply. Additionally, this handbook is packed with unique features to ensure you get the most out of ChatGPT, including:

- **Step-by-step tutorials:** Clear, detailed instructions to guide you through each stage of using the various features of ChatGPT.

- **Visual aids:** Screenshots and illustrations to make tutorials easier to understand.

- **Secret prompt formula:** A proven framework to craft highly effective prompts for maximum results.

- **Ready-to-use prompt formula reference guide:** A handy resource to help you consistently write effective prompts

The tools and the practical framework of this book equip you to build a solid foundation and acquire the practical skills needed to efficiently use ChatGPT and unlock its full potential.

This book will help you learn what ChatGPT is, how it works, and how to set it up. You will discover tricks to craft clear prompts for desired outcomes. The guide uncovers the wide range of applications and potential ChatGPT offers across different fields. It will help you make the most of ChatGPT's capabilities and functionalities as well as tailor its responses and workflows to meet your specific requirements and use cases.

You can actively use ChatGPT as you progress through the guide. Take moments to practice the exercises, experiment with the example prompts I shared, and watch your skills grow. Hands-on learning is the fastest path to mastery; this way, you'll see results almost immediately!

By the end of this book, you will know how to use it to revolutionize your work and daily life. You will be better equipped to approach projects with creativity and confidence, automate repetitive tasks, and dramatically boost your productivity. Best of all, you will have the tools and knowledge to save hours each week and free up time to focus on other aspects of your life.

Are you ready to master this secret weapon for success? Dive right in and discover its full potential!

Chapter 1:
What Is ChatGPT?

Let's imagine, for a moment, that you have a personal assistant available all day and night to answer your questions and help with creative projects or other tasks. Wouldn't that make life much simpler?

We are already living in that reality, thanks to OpenAI. ChatGPT is a conversational AI assistant developed by OpenAI and all one needs to do is type instructions into the chat field, and it will generate a response tailored to the request. Now, isn't that awesome?

ChatGPT's primary purpose is to assist with tasks, provide information, and inspire creativity in both personal and professional contexts. It's a smart tool that's been instrumental in supporting data analysis, formulating clinical trial protocols, and designing scientific studies to streamline research processes (Islam et al., 2023).

The assistant is also used in higher education to enhance learning experiences by assisting in the creation of assessments, generating essays, and facilitating language translation, thereby supporting both students and educators (Dempere et al., 2023).

This shows how powerful the super tool is, but there's so much more it can do! You can turn to it if you need help writing an email, brainstorming fresh ideas, or even preparing a shopping list.

But how does ChatGPT work, and what exactly can it do? Let's explore.

What ChatGPT Can Do

Research projects the conversational AI market, including ChatGPT, to grow exponentially, reaching $32.62 billion by 2030 (Grand View Research, 2023). To get a picture of what ChatGPT can do, it's best to see it in action. Here are three practical examples that showcase its capabilities.

Writing Emails

If you need to create a professional email for setting up a meeting to discuss a presentation next week but aren't sure how to word it, ChatGPT can! The tool can help you draft a clear email and save you time and effort, as shown in the following image. The instructions entered into ChatGPT are displayed on the right side in the gray text field. On the left side, you'll find the response that ChatGPT generated.

> Please write an email to my colleague to fix a meeting to discuss our presentation next week.

Subject: Meeting to Discuss Upcoming Presentation

Hi [Colleague's Name],

I hope you're doing well. I wanted to arrange a time to go over the details for our presentation scheduled for next week. It would be great to ensure we're aligned on key points and structure, so we can deliver a strong presentation together.

Could you let me know your availability over the next few days? I'm flexible and can work around your schedule to find a convenient time for both of us.

Looking forward to collaborating on this!

Best,
[Your Name]

Apple Pie Recipe and Shopping List

Thinking about baking a delicious apple pie? ChatGPT can generate a detailed shopping list with all the ingredients you'll need and create a visual image for inspiration to bring your dessert to life. ChatGPT can even provide a step-by-step recipe for baking the perfect apple pie!

> I have flour, six eggs, sugar, salt, and six apples at home for baking. I want to make an apple pie. Please create a shopping list of the missing ingredients and generate an image of a tasty apple pie.

Here's a delightful image of a freshly baked apple pie to inspire your baking!

Shopping List for Missing Ingredients:

1. **Unsalted butter** (1 cup or 2 sticks, for making the pie crust)
2. **Ground cinnamon** (1 teaspoon, to flavor the apple filling)
3. **Brown sugar** (optional, 1/4 cup, for a richer filling)
4. **Lemon juice** (optional, 1 tablespoon, to enhance the flavor of the apples)
5. **Ice water** (if not already available, for preparing the pie dough)

With these additions, you'll have everything you need to make a delicious homemade apple pie!

Business Report With Graphs

For work, you may need to create a business report, complete with illustrations and graphs. ChatGPT can draft the content for your report and also visualize the data.

> Please give me Apple's last five yearly business reports in a list including critical indicators.

Here is a summary of Apple's key financial indicators over the past five fiscal years:

Fiscal Year	Revenue (USD billions)	Net Income (USD billions)	Earnings Per Share (USD)	Gross Margin (%)
2023	383.3	97.0	6.13	44.1
2022	394.3	99.8	6.11	43.3
2021	365.8	94.7	5.61	41.8
2020	274.5	57.4	3.28	38.2
2019	260.2	55.3	2.97	37.8

These figures are derived from Apple's annual reports and financial statements. For detailed information, you can refer to Apple's Investor Relations page. APPLE INVESTOR RELATIONS

Quellen

> Please visualize this data with four graphs showing the increasing years on the horizontal axis (only years without comma) and the values on the vertical axis starting from zero.

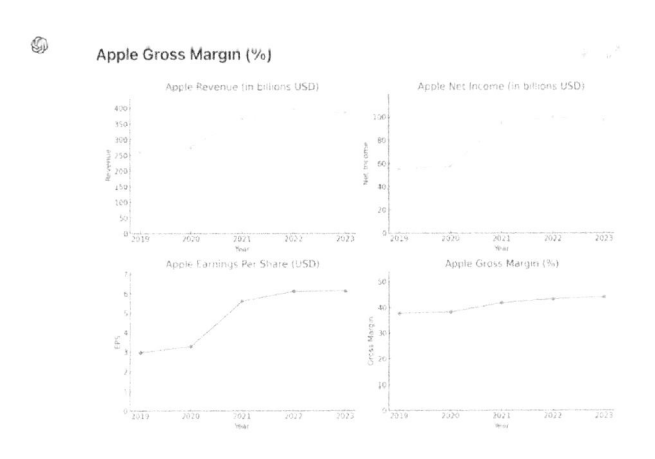

Apple Gross Margin (%)

Apple Revenue (in billions USD)

Apple Net Income (in billions USD)

Apple Earnings Per Share (USD)

Apple Gross Margin (%)

These examples demonstrate ChatGPT's versatility and how it effortlessly adapts to personal, educational, or professional needs. Its capabilities extend beyond generating text-based responses because you can also use it to create images, graphs, and tables, which makes it a comprehensive tool for a wide range of tasks.

The Origins of ChatGPT

All this is exciting and may sound simple, but what ChatGPT can accomplish today is the culmination of years of groundbreaking innovation, extensive research, and continuous refinement in the field of artificial intelligence. To fully appreciate its capabilities, it's worth taking a short moment to explore the origins and evolution of ChatGPT, tracing how this remarkable technology came to be.

About OpenAI

ChatGPT is the brainchild of OpenAI, an organization committed to advancing artificial intelligence (AI) in a safe, ethical, and responsible manner. Founded in 2015 by prominent tech leaders, OpenAI operates with the mission of broadly sharing the benefits of AI across all of humanity. As a pioneer in the field, OpenAI has developed cutting-edge technologies that push the boundaries of what AI can achieve while prioritizing transparency and safety in its research. Their groundbreaking innovations, like GPT (Generative Pre-trained Transformer), have revolutionized the way people interact with AI, making complex technology accessible and practical for everyday use.

OpenAI supports collaboration by sharing research and engaging with the global scientific community, which ensures that progress remains aligned with human values. With an unwavering focus on ethical AI development, OpenAI continues to shape a future where artificial intelligence is a powerful tool for positive societal impact. ChatGPT is just one of the many transformative contributions that OpenAI has brought to the world.

The Evolution of ChatGPT

ChatGPT is part of the groundbreaking series of language models known as GPT. Since the release of GPT-1, each iteration—GPT-2, GPT-3, and beyond—has marked a significant leap in sophistication and functionality. These models have evolved by training on vast and diverse datasets, and that enables them to better understand context, generate coherent text, and mimic human-like communication with remarkable accuracy. GPT-3, in particular, showcased unprecedented versatility and laid the foundation for ChatGPT's advanced capabilities. With the introduction of GPT-4, the model has reached new heights as it now shows improved reasoning, creativity, and adaptability. These advancements make it even more effective for both personal and professional applications. Today, ChatGPT is proof of this evolution as it has transformed how we interact with artificial intelligence.

Having discussed the origin of ChatGPT and the impressive range of tasks it can perform, it's worth taking a moment to delve into the technology that powers it. What makes it so effective? How does it handle everything from simple inquiries to complex problem-solving?

How Does ChatGPT Work?

At its core, ChatGPT is a powerful "language model" designed to understand and generate human-like text by analyzing patterns in language. It is built on the Generative Pre-trained Transformer (GPT) architecture, which processes massive datasets of text to learn the relationships between words, phrases, and context. ChatGPT can generate coherent, contextually relevant, and creative responses to a wide range of inputs by leveraging this knowledge. The model uses advanced algorithms to predict the next word in a sequence, which enables it to simulate natural conversations and assist with complex tasks. This blend of deep learning and language processing makes ChatGPT an incredibly versatile tool for communication and problem-solving.

Neural Networks Made Simple

Neural networks form the foundation of ChatGPT and empower it to process and generate language in a way that mimics human communication. These networks are inspired by the structure of the human brain, using layers of interconnected nodes to analyze and learn from vast amounts of text data. ChatGPT generates coherent and contextually relevant responses by identifying patterns, relationships, and context within the data.

In essence, the technology behind ChatGPT combines cutting-edge neural networks with advanced language modeling to create a system that feels both intuitive and responsive. This seamless integration of deep learning and natural language processing is what empowers ChatGPT to assist users across a wide range of tasks with remarkable accuracy and adaptability.

Misconceptions About ChatGPT

As powerful as ChatGPT is, it's essential to understand its limitations so that you can use it effectively. While the model often feels human-like in its responses, this can sometimes lead to misunderstandings about what it is and how it operates. Here are some facts to clarify common misconceptions about ChatGPT:

- **ChatGPT doesn't "think:"** While it might seem as though the model is reasoning or making decisions, it's simply analyzing patterns in the vast dataset on which it was trained. It predicts the next word or phrase based on context, but does not possess independent thought, reasoning, or understanding like a human.

- **It's not infallible:** Despite its impressive abilities, ChatGPT can produce incorrect, misleading, or irrelevant answers. These errors arise because the model doesn't truly understand the content; it merely generates text based on probabilities. It is crucial to verify the information and analyze it with a human mind when using ChatGPT for critical tasks.

- **It learns from patterns, not intent:** While its responses can feel intentional or emotionally aware, ChatGPT lacks emotions, intent, or awareness. It mimics conversational tone and style but does not have any underlying understanding of the meaning or context behind its outputs.

- **It's not self-learning:** Unlike human beings, ChatGPT doesn't learn dynamically by interacting with users. Its capabilities are static, defined by the training it received prior to deployment, but OpenAI can improve ChatGPT's performance through updates and fine-tuning with new datasets or feedback.

Understanding these nuances helps set realistic expectations and sets the stage for you to use ChatGPT responsibly.

Now that you know what ChatGPT is and have a glimpse of its impressive capabilities, the next big step is learning how to use it, so let's get right into it!

Chapter 2:
Getting Started With ChatGPT

Setting up ChatGPT is easier than making a cup of coffee but a lot more exciting. In just a few clicks, you can unlock a world of streamlined workflows and creative breakthroughs!

In this chapter, we'll guide you step-by-step through setting up your account, starting your first conversation, and navigating the intuitive interface. It's now time to get practical because to truly comprehend the power of ChatGPT, you have to engage with it directly. As we progress through this and the following chapters, you will work hands on with ChatGPT, experimenting with its features and exploring its capabilities through practical examples. By the end of this chapter, you should feel more confident when exploring ChatGPT, as you will be fully equipped to unlock its powerful features. Let's get started!

Setting Up Your ChatGPT Account

To get started, visit chatgpt.com, where you will land on the homepage featuring a central prompt input field, which looks as follows.

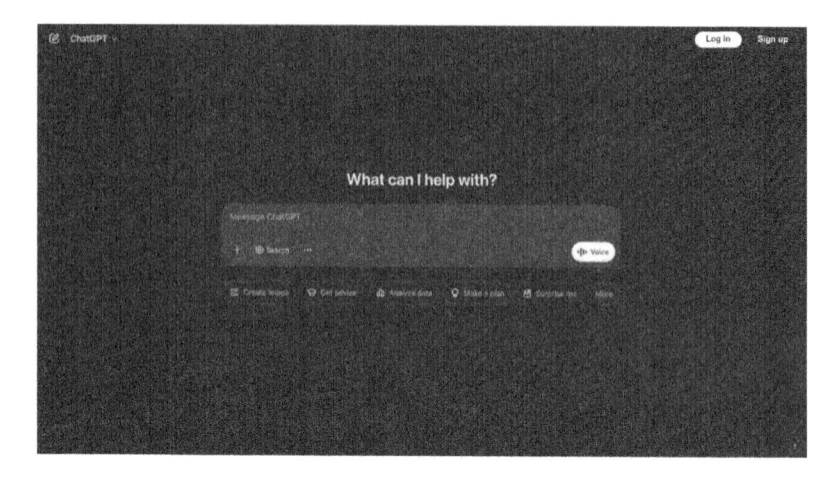

Here, you can immediately begin using the free version of ChatGPT. However, it's best to create an account first or log in if you already have one to unlock features essential for this handbook, such as saving chat history for future reference, accessing more advanced responses, and improving your overall experience.

Creating an Account

Follow these simple steps to set up your account:

1. Click on the Sign-up button on the top right corner of the homepage.

2. Choose your preferred login method, such as Google, Microsoft, or Apple, or create an account using your email address.

3. Complete the registration process by verifying your email and setting a password.

Once you've created an account and logged in, you are all set to start using ChatGPT.

Starting Your First Conversation

Once logged in, you'll see the ChatGPT interface, featuring a central prompt input field. If you haven't customized the appearance yet, the default theme will likely be set to black.

What can I help with?

To start, we will enter a first prompt. A "prompt" is simply a question or task you ask ChatGPT to respond to. Now, type the following prompt in the input field: *"List five ways AI can improve my daily routine."* Here's what the screen might look like:

What can I help with?

List five ways AI can improve my daily routine.

After entering your prompt, press "Enter" or click on the arrow icon to send your prompt and receive your first response from ChatGPT.

> List five ways AI can improve my daily routine.

1. **Automates Routine Tasks**
   AI can handle tasks like sorting emails, scheduling meetings, or setting reminders, freeing up your time for more important activities.

2. **Enhances Productivity**
   Tools powered by AI can prioritize your to-do list and recommend the most efficient ways to complete tasks based on your schedule.

3. **Improves Health Tracking**
   AI-driven apps and wearables monitor your fitness, sleep, and diet, providing personalized recommendations to maintain a healthy lifestyle.

4. **Supports Learning**
   Platforms with AI adapt to your pace and preferences, offering tailored courses or resources to help you acquire new skills effectively.

5. **Simplifies Decision-Making**
   AI analyzes data to suggest solutions, such as budgeting apps that optimize finances or meal planners that use available ingredients.

As we can observe, ChatGPT automatically generates responses that are well-structured, often featuring clear headings and numbered lists.

Sample Prompts to Try

To get an idea of how ChatGPT responds, try out these examples:

- *"Provide a quick summary of Shakespeare's Romeo and Juliet."*

- *"Suggest three healthy lunch ideas I can make in under 15 minutes."*

- *"Summarize AI in three sentences."*

Feel free to use follow-up prompts to refine its responses. For example, if you ask for lunch ideas, you can follow up with, *"Can you make it vegetarian?"* Similarly, if you'd like the response formatted differently or expanded, you can instruct ChatGPT with prompts like, *"Format this in bullet points and add two more sentences."* ChatGPT takes this follow-up prompt into account and adjusts the response accordingly, as you can see in the following example:

> Summarize AI in three sentences.

AI, or Artificial Intelligence, allows machines to simulate human intelligence in tasks like learning and decision-making. It relies on data and algorithms to recognize patterns and make predictions. AI is used in applications like virtual assistants, recommendation systems, and autonomous vehicles.

> Format in bullet points and add two more sentences.

- AI, or Artificial Intelligence, enables machines to mimic human intelligence in tasks such as learning and decision-making.
- It uses data and algorithms to identify patterns, make predictions, and improve over time.
- Common applications of AI include virtual assistants, recommendation systems, and autonomous vehicles.
- AI can also automate repetitive tasks, freeing up human resources for more complex work.
- As AI evolves, it continues to impact industries from healthcare and finance to education and transportation.

Now, give it a try by experimenting with your prompts and refining your responses through follow-up questions.

Navigating the ChatGPT Interface

Before diving into the full potential of ChatGPT, it's important to get familiar with its interface. The platform is designed to be intuitive and user-friendly, with all key features easily accessible. This section will guide you through the essential elements of the

ChatGPT interface to ensure you can explore it with ease. The main ChatGPT Interface consists of the following elements illustrated in the image below.

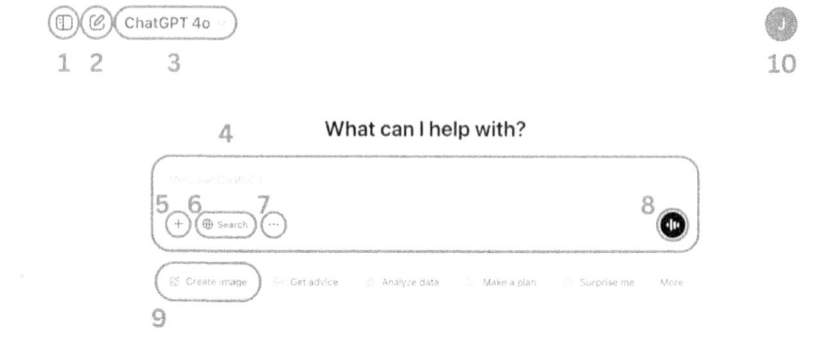

Here is a list of the different elements:

1. open sidebar

2. new chat

3. choosing the model

4. prompt input field

5. attach files

6. search the web

7. view tools

8. use voice mode

9. prompt recommendations

10. account and settings

18

11. help and information

In the following part, we delve deeper into each of these functions.

Open Sidebar

Clicking on this icon will open the sidebar, which looks like the following illustration.

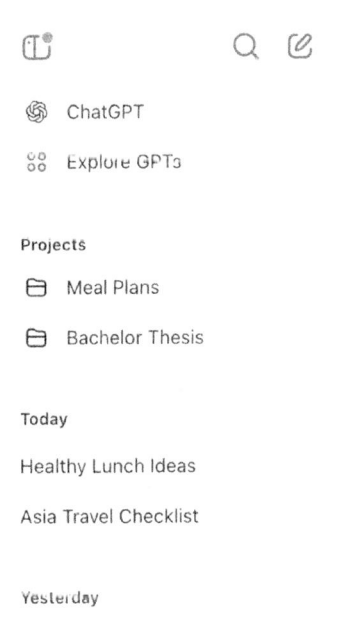

ChatGPT

Explore GPTs

Projects

Meal Plans

Bachelor Thesis

Today

Healthy Lunch Ideas

Asia Travel Checklist

Yesterday

The sidebar allows us to do four main things:

- **Explore GPTs:** This function enables us to access and manage different GPTs you've created by your own or other ChatGPT users and select the one you want to use. We'll dive deeper into this feature in Chapter 11.

19

- **Projects:** With this function, multiple conversations can be saved within a project to maintain order among various conversations.

- **Conversation history:** Here, you can easily view and manage your recent chats, allowing you to revisit or continue past conversations.

- **Search chats:** The icon with the magnifying glass gives us the possibility to search directly for keywords and past conversations.

New Chat

This icon starts a new chat. You can click here when you want to begin a new conversation on a different topic. It helps you keep your discussions organized, which makes it easier to locate specific responses in your chat history.

Choosing the Model

As mentioned earlier, ChatGPT provides various models to cater to different needs. At the time of writing, the models visualized in the following image are available:

ChatGPT 4o ⌄

Model

GPT-4o ✓
Great for most questions

GPT-4o with scheduled tasks BETA
Ask ChatGPT to follow up later

o1
Uses advanced reasoning

o3-mini
Fast at advanced reasoning

o3-mini-high
Great at coding and logic

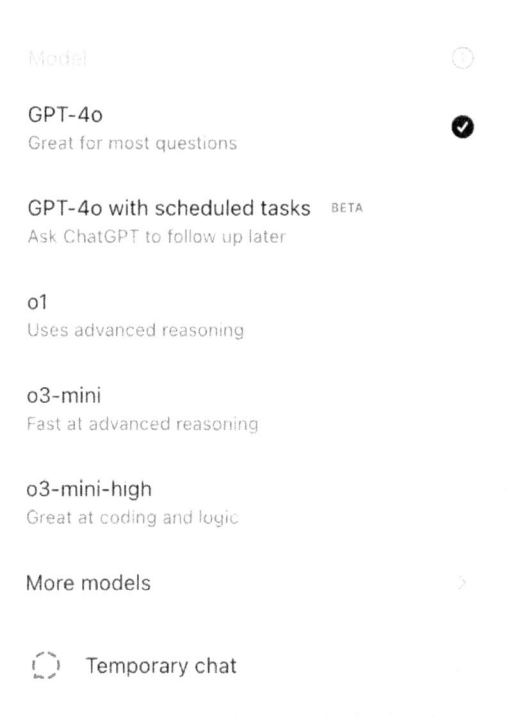

More models >

◯ Temporary chat

The most important ones are:

- **GPT-4o:** A versatile option suitable for most tasks. It excels in web searches, file uploads, and general problem-solving, and that makes it a reliable choice for everyday use.

- **o1:** An advanced reasoning model designed for complex tasks in fields like science, coding, and mathematics. While it offers deep analytical capabilities, it lacks certain utility features like web browsing. Additionally, it takes longer to generate responses due to its focus on in-depth reasoning. For most typical use cases, GPT-4o is the more efficient and capable option.

- **o3-mini:** A specialized model for technical domains that require both precision and speed. It is the newest and most cost-efficient option in the reasoning series, balancing accuracy with quick response times. Unlike o1, this model supports web searches.

- **o3-mini-high:** A more advanced version of o3-mini, offering higher intelligence and improved logical reasoning. While it takes slightly longer to process responses, it is particularly well-suited for coding and analytical tasks.

ChatGPT models evolve rapidly as OpenAI continuously improves their capabilities and develops new features. It's not uncommon for new models to be introduced or existing ones to be upgraded often. Therefore, it is possible that these models above, which were used at the time of writing this book, may not be the version you are using. For the purposes of this guide, we recommend using the GPT-4o model, which provides the features and performance needed for most scenarios outlined in this book.

Prompt Input Field

This is where you type your questions or tasks, and then you send your prompt by pressing Enter.

Attaching Files

This feature allows you to upload files for ChatGPT to analyze and work with. You can use it for tasks such as summarizing documents, analyzing data, or interpreting images, which makes the tool powerful for efficiently handling complex information. We will explore this functionality in greater detail in Chapter 6.

Search the Web

This feature allows ChatGPT to access live information from the web, which is a useful expansion of its capabilities. We will have a closer look at this feature in Chapter 5.

View Tools

Here you get access to additional tools such as image generation or canvas for editing text directly with ChatGPT.

Use Voice Mode

With ChatGPT, you can engage in a natural conversation using your voice, just as you would when interacting with a voice assistant. While in Voice Mode, ChatGPT automatically generates a transcript of your conversation in real-time. We will delve into more about this in Chapter 8.

Recommendations for Prompts

This section provides a variety of prompt recommendations to help you get started and explore what ChatGPT is capable of.

Account and Settings

This icon located in the top-right corner will open up the Account and Settings window:

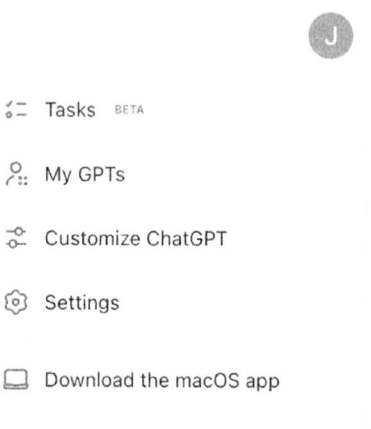

- Tasks BETA
- My GPTs
- Customize ChatGPT
- Settings
- Download the macOS app
- Upgrade Plan
- Get ChatGPT search extension
- Log out

This window lets you do the following:

- **Tasks:** This section introduces the tasks feature, allowing ChatGPT to perform actions for you in the future.

- **My GPTs:** This section lets you create your own GPT. While we'll dive deeper into this in Chapter 11, know that you can design your own GPTs tailored to specific needs, and that's great for businesses or specialized tasks.

24

- **Customize ChatGPT:** In this section, you can personalize how ChatGPT interacts with you. We'll explore this in detail in Chapter 10.

- **Settings:** Here, you can access the settings menu, which appears as follows:

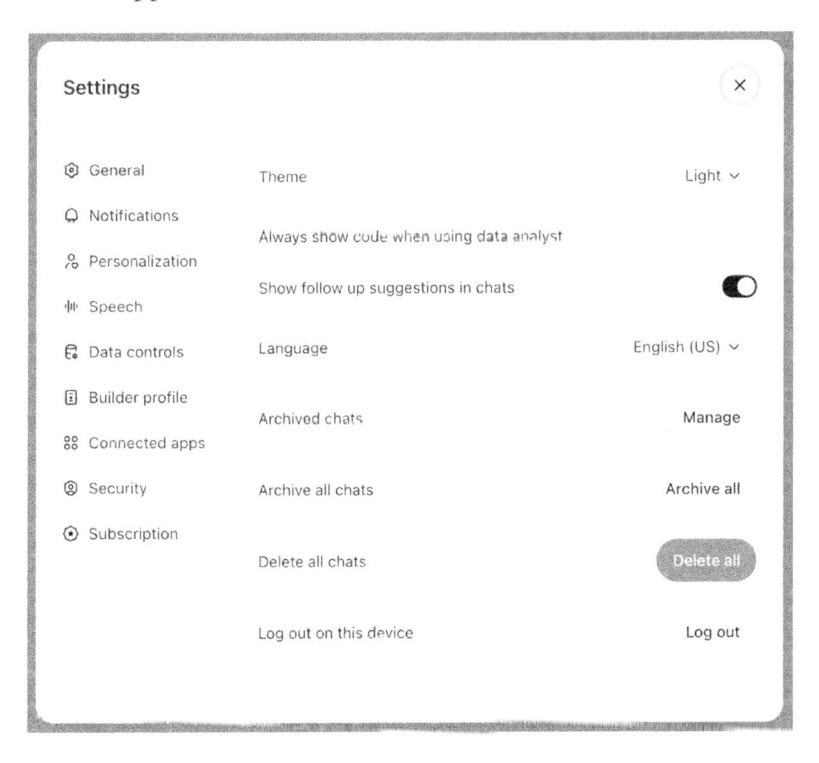

Settings			✕
⚙ General	Theme		Light ⌄
🔔 Notifications	Always show code when using data analyst		
⚙ Personalization	Show follow up suggestions in chats		🔘
🎙 Speech			
🗄 Data controls	Language		English (US) ⌄
📋 Builder profile	Archived chats		Manage
🔗 Connected apps			
🛡 Security	Archive all chats		Archive all
⊙ Subscription			
	Delete all chats		Delete all
	Log out on this device		Log out

In the settings menu, you can customize various options to suit your preferences. Under the section "Personalization," you can manage ChatGPT's memory—a feature we will explore in more detail in Chapter 10.

25

Help and Information

Click the question mark in the bottom-right corner for various functions such as tutorials, FAQs, and Keyboard Shortcuts.

- Help & FAQ
- Release notes
- Terms & policies
- Keyboard shortcuts
- Report Illegal Content

Choosing the Right ChatGPT Subscription Model

To set you up for the following chapters, let's explore the subscription models that ChatGPT offers. You can access and adjust these through the "Account and Settings" menu by selecting the "Upgrade Plan" option. ChatGPT offers several subscription models to fit different needs. Here's a quick overview:

- **Free plan:** Access basic ChatGPT features (GPT-4.0 Mini) for casual use.

- **Plus plan ($20/month):** Unlock advanced features like GPT-4 capabilities and priority access during high traffic.

- **Team plan ($25 per user/month):** Designed for collaborative teams with shared access.

- **Enterprise (Custom pricing):** Tailored solutions for businesses requiring large-scale use.

For beginners, the Free Plan provides a simple way to explore the platform's core features. However, it is limited to basic functionalities and does not include advanced tools like image generation. To fully benefit from this guide and unlock ChatGPT's advanced capabilities, such as image generation, you may want to start with the Plus Plan. It's an excellent choice for beginners looking to get the most out of ChatGPT while exploring its full potential.

Now that your account is ready and your first prompts are in the books, you're already on your way to becoming a ChatGPT pro. Next, let's refine how you communicate with this tool to achieve extraordinary results.

Chapter 3:
Mastering Prompt Engineering

ChatGPT is only as good as the prompts you provide it. Crafting functional prompts that are clear, specific, and tailored to your needs is the key to unlocking its full potential. In this chapter, you'll learn how to design prompts that consistently produce accurate and useful responses. With a mix of principles, techniques, and real-world examples, you'll gain the skills to constructively communicate with AI, ensuring it delivers results that meet your expectations.

What Is Prompt Engineering?

We already established that a prompt is simply the input or question you provide to ChatGPT. It is the instruction that guides how ChatGPT responds. Whether you're asking for a recipe, requesting an explanation, or drafting an email, the quality of the prompt directly influences the quality of the response. Now, prompt engineering is the art of creating inputs that maximize accuracy and relevance in how ChatGPT responds. Why does it matter? Because the output depends on the input. A vague or poorly constructed prompt can result in generic or unclear responses, while a well-crafted prompt yields relevance. Here are two examples:

- **Simple prompt:** *"Write a story."*

- **Improved prompt:** *"Write a 500-word short story about a young detective solving their first case, using a humorous tone and featuring an unexpected twist."*

In the following section, we focus on how to improve your prompts to receive better, more accurate responses.

Guidelines for Crafting Effective Prompts

One first option to improve the productivity of your prompts is to adhere to certain guidelines. The following basic principles will help you create prompts that deliver more accurate results:

- **Clarity:** Be specific and unambiguous. Instead of: *"Give advice on starting a business."* Try: *"List three essential steps to start a small online business."*

- **Conciseness:** Keep your prompts focused, avoiding unnecessary words. Instead of: *"Can you maybe tell me some healthy food ideas that don't take too long to prepare?"* Try: *"Suggest three healthy meals that can be made in under 15 minutes."*

- **Detail:** Include relevant information to guide the response. Instead of: *"Help me write a blog post."* Try: *"Write a 300-word blog post about sustainable travel tips for budget-conscious backpackers."*

- **Structure:** Implement a clear structure within your prompt to guide the response effectively. For example: *"Write an inspiring speech about the first man on the Moon. Include the following information: the rocket's immense power, the journey's duration, and the time spent on the Moon. Make it engaging, emotional, and awe-inspiring."*

- **Context:** Provide background information if needed. For example: *"I'm planning a trip to Europe for the first time. Suggest a two-week itinerary with must-see cities."*

Using the Secret Prompt Formula

Another proven way to craft extremely effective prompts is by using a structured prompt formula. The Prompt formula consists of specific components, each designed to contribute to a tailored and precise outcome. After experimenting with thousands of prompts, I discovered a secret prompt formula that consistently delivers the most accurate and reliable results for me. Here's the secret prompt formula with its different components:

[Role] + [Task] + [Context] + [Target Audience] + [Style] + [Format]

To apply the secret prompt formula, we craft our prompts following this structure, incorporating each component. Below is a demonstration to create a pasta recipe:

Role	*"You are a professional chef.*
Task	*Write an easy-to-follow recipe for a classic pasta dish.*
Context	*The dish should be simple to prepare and beginner-friendly.*
Target audience	*For busy college students who want a quick, nutritious meal.*
Style	*Use a friendly, encouraging tone with simple language.*
Format	*Provide the recipe in bullet points with each step numbered, including a short list of ingredients and estimated prep or cook time."*

Including each of these components provides ChatGPT with highly precise instructions that result in exceptional responses. Now, let's break down the formula and examine each component in detail.

Role

The "role" in a prompt defines the perspective or expertise ChatGPT should adopt while responding. When you specify a role, you guide the AI to tailor its tone, style, and knowledge to suit that specific domain or profession, which makes the response more relevant and authentic.

Examples:

- *You are a professional chef.*

- *You are an experienced digital marketing copywriter.*

- *You are a life coach specializing in stress management.*

Task

The "task" outlines the specific action or objective you want ChatGPT to accomplish. Clearly stating the task ensures the AI understands the goal and provides a focused, actionable response.

Examples:

- *Write an easy-to-follow recipe for a classic pasta dish.*

- *Summarize the key points of this article.*

- *Suggest five creative marketing ideas for a small business.*

Context

The "context" provides additional background or relevant details to help ChatGPT tailor its response. Including specifics ensures the AI generates a response that aligns closely with your situation or needs.

Examples:

- *The dish should be simple to prepare and beginner-friendly.*

- *I will travel to Asia for the first time. It will be the rainy season, and I want to take diving lessons.*

- *The business is a local coffee shop looking to attract more young customers.*

Target Audience

The "target audience" defines who the response is intended for, which helps make sure it is appropriately tailored in tone, language, and content. Specifying the audience helps ChatGPT craft a message that resonates with and meets the needs of the intended group.

Examples:

- *For busy college students who want a quick, nutritious meal.*

- *The target audience is small business owners looking to improve their online presence.*

- *The reader is a beginner in the kitchen with limited cooking experience.*

Style

The "style" describes the tone or manner in which ChatGPT should deliver the response. Resultantly, this shapes how the message feels to the reader. Specifying the style helps make certain that the output aligns with the desired mood or approach for the situation.

Examples:

- *Use a friendly, encouraging tone with simple language.*
- *Adopt a persuasive and professional tone.*
- *Explain it in a commanding tone like issuing decisive commands in a military briefing.*

Format

The "format" outlines the structure or organization of the response, ensuring clarity and suitability for the intended purpose. Inputting the format helps ChatGPT deliver information the way you want it presented.

Examples:

- *Provide the recipe in bullet points with each step numbered.*
- *Write a 500-word essay with an introduction, body, and conclusion.*
- *Summarize in three sentences.*

For more examples of each component, refer to **The Ready-To-Use Prompt Formula Reference Guide** located at the end of this handbook.

In order to see how the prompt formula looks in action, here are two more example prompts according to the prompt formula:

Example prompt 1

Role	*"You are an experienced digital marketing copywriter.*
Task	*Write compelling copy for an online course about programming.*
Context	*The course is beginner-friendly and covers Python basics.*
Target audience	*Young professionals and college students looking to build new skills.*
Style	*Use an engaging, motivational tone.*
Format	*Provide a headline, a brief introduction, and three bullet points highlighting key benefits."*

Example prompt 2

Role	*"You are a rocket science physicist.*
Task	*Explain how a rocket engine works.*
Context	*The goal is to have the explanation featured in the fun section of a science magazine, making it entertaining and humorous while still providing an accurate overview of rocket science principles.*

Target audience	*Our target audience is professionals, especially those who appreciate a lighthearted take on complex topics.*
Style	*Use a tone and language similar to Donald Trump, emphasizing a larger-than-life, confident style with exaggerations and memorable phrases.*
Format	*Present the explanation in a rhyming poem, aiming for about 500 words to fully capture the nuances of rocket science in an entertaining way."*

Now, try using these two examples of our secret prompt formula. Write them into your prompt input field and see how accurate the results turn out. Once you've tested them, challenge yourself to get comfortable with the formula by creating your own prompts. This hands-on practice will help you master the structure and unlock its full potential. For your convenience, this book includes a **Ready-To-Use Prompt Formula Reference Guide** at the end, which features numerous examples of each component of the prompt structure. You can use this guide as a handy reference and a source of inspiration to craft your own prompts productively and tailor them according to this formula.

Using the prompt formula is excellent for achieving accurate and detailed results. However, shorter prompts can also yield the desired outcome in many cases. Since writing each prompt according to the formula can be time-consuming, it may make sense to deviate from it at times. A good practice is to start with a short, concise prompt without necessarily using the formula and see if it produces the result you need. If it doesn't, you can refine and expand your input using the formula for greater precision. Additionally, remember that the formula is flexible, so you can adapt it by omitting certain parts while still maintaining its effectiveness. This approach allows you to strike a balance between simplicity and detail, depending on your needs.

Tips for Effective Prompting

Mastering effective prompting is a process. When you adhere to certain rules, you will be able to improve the results that ChatGPT generates. In the following section, we'll explore a range of tips and strategies designed to help you communicate more constructively with ChatGPT.

Break Down Prompts

Overloading a prompt with multiple questions at once can lead to diluted or confusing responses. Instead, it is important to focus on asking one question or completing one task at a time. For example, instead of asking, *"What is AI, how can it help businesses, and what are its limitations?"* break it into individual prompts, such as:

- *"What is AI?"*
- *"How can AI help businesses?"*
- *"What are the limitations of AI?"*

Breaking down prompts helps ChatGPT provide clear, focused answers to each question.

Summarize Long Documents in Sections

When dealing with lengthy documents, it can be overwhelming to process all the information at once. To constructively manage this, break the content into smaller, manageable sections and ask ChatGPT to summarize each part individually. Focusing on one section at a time allows for greater accuracy and helps ensure that you do not overlook any critical details you or the tool might make.

Here's how:

1. Upload one chapter to ChatGPT and ask: *"Summarize the main points of this chapter."*
2. Copy the summary into a final summary document.
3. Repeat for all chapters and combine these summaries into a cohesive overview to provide a comprehensive understanding of the document as a whole.

Ask for Missing Information

To get the result you're looking for, it can be incredibly useful to ask ChatGPT what additional details it might need to make its response more accurate. This is especially valuable for tasks that require specific context or nuanced instructions. Simply prompt the tool to identify the missing information necessary for effectively completing a specific task. For example: *"I want to bake a cake. What additional information do you need from me?"*

ChatGPT might ask about the type of cake, your available ingredients, or your baking skill level.

Similarly, if your initial prompt doesn't deliver the desired result, follow up by asking, *"What kind of information would improve your response?"* This collaborative approach ensures a more refined and tailored output.

Provide Examples

When you want ChatGPT to adopt a specific tone, style, or format, you may find it constructive to provide an example that will help improve the response. Examples give clear references and help ChatGPT understand exactly what you are aiming for. This demonstration helps ensure the output aligns with your expectations. For instance, you could say:

"Write a blog post introduction in a friendly, conversational tone, similar to this: [Insert Example]."

When you include a sample, you reduce guesswork and make it easier for ChatGPT to mimic the desired approach.

Use Delimiters

Delimiters are symbols or markers used to define specific sections of text, which makes your prompts clearer and easier for ChatGPT to interpret. They help organize the input by separating important parts to allow the AI to focus precisely on the task at hand. Delimiters are particularly useful for distinguishing between example text or text that needs to be adjusted and the actual commands or instructions.

Common delimiters include triple quotes (""""), XML tags (<tag> </tag>), or labeled sections like "Title:" and "Subtitle:" Here are two examples demonstrating how to use delimiters to distinguish between a command or query and the accompanying example or text for ChatGPT to process.

Example: *"Summarize the text delimited by triple quotes in three sentences: """"[Insert text here]"""."*

Example: *"Translate the title to French. Title: Write the best blog post ever."*

Delimiters let ChatGPT know exactly where to find the relevant text, and that improves accuracy and reduces ambiguity, especially when working with complex or lengthy inputs.

View Prompting as an Iterative Process

Prompting is rarely a one-and-done activity. Try thinking of it as an iterative process. Don't hesitate to experiment, ask follow-up questions, or reformulate your prompts if the initial response does not meet your expectations. Analyze what might have gone wrong, adjust your instructions, and try again to refine the output. For instance, if a response feels too vague, you can follow up by asking ChatGPT to clarify or expand on specific points. This trial-and-error approach improves the quality of responses and also helps you master the art of crafting precise and effective prompts over time.

In addition, ChatGPT provides a convenient feature that allows you to easily modify specific parts of a response. Instead of rewriting the entire prompt to generate a completely new response, you can focus on adjusting just the part you want to refine. Simply highlight the section you'd like to change, click on the quotation mark icon, and enter a new prompt to guide the revision, as demonstrated in the next two illustrations.

> Write a short text about volcanos

⑤ Volcanoes are openings in the Earth's crust where magma, gases, and ash erupt from deep below the surfa 99 ney can form mountains, islands, or craters over time through repeated eruptions. Famous examples include Mount Vesuvius in Italy and Mount Fuji in Japan. While eruptions can be destructive, they also create fertile soil and new land, showcasing the Earth's power and its role in shaping our planet's surface.

> "examples include Mount Vesuvius in Italy and Mount Fuji in Japan"

Please add a third example.

This makes it simple to tailor the output to your exact needs without redoing the entire response.

Reuse Effective Prompts

When you find a prompt that works exceptionally well, save it as a reusable template for future tasks. This saves time and also ensures consistency in the quality of your results. Over time, build a collection of effective prompts and organize them by tasks or use cases, such as writing, summarizing, brainstorming, or translating. As you continue to experiment, regularly refine and expand your library to include new variations or improvements based on what works best. Having a go-to set of prompts makes your workflow more efficient and helps you achieve consistent, high-quality outcomes with ChatGPT.

Think of prompting as a skill that evolves. Consistently experimenting and refining your approach gradually enhances your ability to craft effective prompts and achieve better results. Even when outputs are incomplete or not as expected, take them as valuable learning opportunities to identify areas for improvement and fine-tune your technique.

For more advanced tips and resources on prompting, visit the OpenAI website.

Now that you've mastered how to ask the right questions, it's time to see how ChatGPT can take over your workload. In the following chapter, let's explore its practical applications and uncover how it can revolutionize your daily life.

Chapter 4:
Practical Applications of ChatGPT

Research shows organizations using AI tools report a 40% improvement in productivity across repetitive and creative tasks (Chui et al., 2023).

This means that you, too, can outsource tedious tasks and do more with less effort. ChatGPT has your back!

This versatile assistant is more than a conversational tool because it's designed to streamline your tasks, boost your productivity, and spark your creativity. In this chapter, we'll dive into the many practical ways you can integrate ChatGPT into your daily life and professional activities. Whether you're looking to automate repetitive tasks, tackle complex projects, or generate innovative ideas, this chapter reveals actionable examples and prompts to help you unlock the full potential of ChatGPT.

By the end of this chapter, you'll have a clear understanding of how you can leverage ChatGPT for automating tasks and enhancing productivity, both personally and professionally. From managing your schedule to brainstorming creative content, the possibilities are virtually endless. Below, you'll find a variety of ideas and sample prompts showcasing potential applications and use cases for ChatGPT. Use these examples as inspiration to explore what's possible. If a particular prompt aligns with your needs, give it a try! Experimentation is an essential part of this learning process, so it's best to start with prompts that interest you, tweak them as necessary and refine them to achieve the best outcomes. With practice, you'll discover just how much ChatGPT can simplify your life!

Writing

ChatGPT is a large language model designed to analyze vast amounts of text and written resources. Its true strength lies in its ability to process, understand, and generate coherent and contextually appropriate text. This makes it an invaluable tool for helping you to write. Whether you're an author crafting compelling stories, drafting professional emails, or simply looking for help with formulating ideas, this efficient tool will help guide you. Here are some practical use cases.

Email Drafting and Response Assistance

ChatGPT crafts professional emails, and personal responses customized to your tone and intent. It ensures your message is clear, polished, and ready to send with minimal effort. This means it gives you room to save time and communicate effectively without compromising quality.

Example: *"Draft a follow-up email to a potential client thanking them for their time and highlighting our key services."*

Example: *"[insert email] This is the email I got. Please draft a replying email to this."*

Storytelling and Creative Writing

Unleash creativity with engaging plots, compelling characters, and detailed outlines for your projects. You may be looking to overcome writer's block or seeking fresh inspiration. ChatGPT sparks unique storytelling ideas tailored to your vision.

Example: *"Create a short story outline about a time traveler discovering a hidden civilization."*

Writing Assistance and Editing

You can enhance your writing with improved grammar, refined sentence structure, and polished style. ChatGPT can paraphrase text, changing it the way you want it.

Example: *"Paraphrase this sentence to make it more concise: [insert sentence]"*

Example: *"[Insert section]. Enhance this section by adding two additional sentences and rewriting it with a more captivating and engaging tone."*

Resume and Cover Letter Writing

ChatGPT lets you create tailored resumes and compelling cover letters that align with specific job descriptions. The tool can assist you in highlighting your strengths, skills, and achievements to make a lasting impression on potential employers.

Example: *"Write a cover letter for a marketing manager position emphasizing creativity and leadership skills."*

Speech Writing Assistance

You can also use ChatGPT to craft well-structured speeches tailored to your purpose, from persuasive arguments to motivational messages. It helps you convey your ideas clearly while incorporating personal anecdotes and insights for a more authentic connection with your audience.

Example: *"Draft a motivational speech for a graduation ceremony, focusing on perseverance and hope."*

Social Media Content Creation

ChatGPT is also an invaluable tool for creating engaging social media content, which makes it an essential resource for self-employed professionals, marketers, and influencers.

Post Ideas and Captions

You can count on ChatGPT to help you create captivating posts, attention-grabbing captions, and relevant hashtags for social media platforms like Instagram, Twitter, LinkedIn or Facebook.

Example: *"Write a witty caption for a travel photo featuring the Eiffel Tower."*

Example: *"Suggest five trending hashtags for a post about baking a cheesecake."*

Marketing Campaigns

Develop SEO-optimized product descriptions, compelling taglines, and persuasive ad copy and generate creative campaign concepts that meet the needs of your target audience.

Example: *"Suggest three taglines for a new eco-friendly water bottle brand."*

Brainstorming and Idea Generation

Coming up with original or innovative ideas can often be challenging. ChatGPT is a powerful catalyst for creativity because it offers a wealth of ideas to inspire and guide you. It streamlines the brainstorming process and makes it more productive. Whether you're an entrepreneur, creator, innovator, or consultant, you can leverage ChatGPT's extensive knowledge base to unlock new opportunities and solutions. Here's how:

Business and Product Ideas

Generate innovative business ideas or product features to meet market demands or solve specific problems. This process involves identifying gaps in existing offerings and exploring creative, practical solutions.

Example: *"Brainstorm five innovative app ideas for personal finance management."*

Content Ideation

Effortlessly generate article topics, blog post ideas, or marketing content with ChatGPT. You can align content ideas with your audience's needs and industry trends as a way to boost engagement and drive results.

Example: *"Suggest blog topics related to mental health for a wellness website."*

Soundscaping for Audiobooks and Podcasts

You can also ask ChatGPT to give you ideas on sound effects, background music, or ambient tones to enhance audio projects.

Example: *"Suggest background music and sound effects for a podcast about mystery stories."*

Personalized Gift Ideas

Recommend unique gifts tailored to individual interests and preferences

Example: *"Suggest a unique birthday gift for someone who loves hiking and photography."*

Learning and Tutoring Support

I used to spend hours searching YouTube for the perfect explanatory video on a specific topic. Those days are behind us, thanks to ChatGPT, which can now be your virtual, personal teacher. ChatGPT is a valuable tool for students as well as teachers. Here are some practical ways to use ChatGPT for learning and creating effective learning materials.

Learning Assistance

You can use ChatGPT to get detailed explanations and support for assignments in various subjects such as math, science, and literature. Simplifying complex concepts and providing clear guidance suitable for different learning levels is just one of the tool's many capabilities.

Example: *"Explain the concept of photosynthesis in simple terms for a middle school student."*

Mind Mapping

If you need help organizing thoughts into structured diagrams for brainstorming sessions, ChatGPT's got it!

Example: *"Create a mind map connecting the causes, effects, and solutions for global warming."*

Excel Help

Working with formulas and numbers isn't everyone's cup of tea. ChatGPT can help you tackle such tasks more easily by providing formulas and tips for completing specific Excel functions.

Example: *"Write an Excel formula to calculate the average of numbers in column A."*

Educational Content Creation

Design engaging quizzes, exercises, and instructional materials tailored to various subjects and learning levels. ChatGPT can assist in creating lesson plans, crafting clear explanations for complex topics, generating interactive learning activities, and providing customized study guides. It's a versatile tool for educators and learners alike.

Example: *"Generate a quiz with 10 questions about the American Revolution for high school students."*

Productivity Tools and Advice

Imagine having a personal fitness coach or a nutritionist specifically aligned to your needs. ChatGPT can do that, too! Take a look:

Task and Time Management

With ChatGPT, you can constructively organize your day through tailored task lists, schedules, and productivity plans. The tool can help you prioritize tasks, allocate time blocks, set reminders, and suggest tools or techniques for better time management. You can easily make it your personal assistant for staying organized and achieving your goals.

Example: *"Plan my workday with two hours for meetings, three hours for focused work, and one hour for emails."*

Financial Planning Assistance

Get support with budgeting, saving strategies, and foundational investment planning. ChatGPT can help design personalized budgets, suggest ways to reduce expenses, explore saving plans, and explain basic investment options. It's a resource for making informed financial decisions and achieving your financial goals.

Example: *"Create a monthly budget for a family of four with a $4,000 income."*

Health and Wellness Guidance

ChatGPT can help you set achievable health goals, explore mindfulness practices, design exercise schedules, and offer ideas for maintaining a balanced lifestyle. This way, you can leverage it to assist you in building healthier habits and staying motivated.

Example: *"Suggest a 30-minute workout routine for beginners."*

Recipe Suggestions

Do you have leftover ingredients that you don't know what to do with? You can discover creative meal ideas based on the ingredients on hand. ChatGPT can provide step-by-step recipes, suggest substitutes for missing ingredients, or tailor dishes to fit any dietary preferences and restrictions you may have. You can make it your go-to source for kitchen inspiration.

Example: *"What can I cook with chicken, broccoli, and rice?"*

Learning New Skills

ChatGPT can help you discover and develop new talents. You can explore step-by-step guidance for mastering new hobbies or skills, such as painting, cooking, gardening, or learning to play the guitar.

Example: *"Provide a beginner's guide to learning guitar chords."*

Travel Planning

Planning the perfect trip with detailed itineraries and packing checklists has never been easier. ChatGPT can recommend destinations based on your preferences, suggest activities and local experiences, provide cost-saving travel tips, and even help with booking ideas or cultural insights.

Example: *"Create a 7-day itinerary for a trip to Italy, including must-see landmarks."*

Event Planning

Are you organizing an event but stuck on themes, timelines, or venues? Have ChatGPT draft you some exciting activities recommended, and have your invitation cards in no time!

Example: *"Suggest themes and activities for a child's birthday party."*

Coding Assistance

One of the great features of ChatGPT is its ability to directly process programming code pasted into the input field. This makes it an incredibly versatile tool for developers, learners, and anyone working with code. Here are some practical use cases.

Coding Help and Debugging

If you need support with writing, debugging, and optimizing code across various programming languages, ChatGPT can deliver just that!

The chat assistant can explain complex programming concepts, suggest best practices, assist with algorithm design, and help troubleshoot errors. To do this, all you need to do is copy code into the prompt field and write your prompt.

Example: *"[insert code] debug this Python code snippet for calculating the factorial of a number."*

Learning Programming Languages

ChatGPT can also offer resources and step-by-step guides for learning new programming skills.

Example: *"Explain the basics of loops in Python with examples."*

Diverse Applications

ChatGPT can execute a variety of applications that you might not have considered, so here are some ideas to inspire you.

Interview Preparation

The tool can generate role-specific interview questions and practice responses to help you prepare better. This can make you feel more confident and ready to showcase your skills and qualifications during the interview.

Example: *"Generate five common interview questions for a software developer role and suggest ideal responses."*

Conversation Starters

You can get engaging ideas for starting conversations at networking events or social gatherings. These prompts help you break the ice, build connections, and make a positive impression.

Example: *"What's an effective conversation starter for meeting new people at a networking event?"*

Dream Interpretation

Did you know ChatGPT can provide entertaining insights into dream symbols and meanings?

Example: *"What does dreaming about flying mean?"*

Meditations and Visualizations

Discover personalized meditation scripts or visualization exercises for relaxation.

Example: *"Write a 10-minute guided meditation for relaxation and stress relief."*

These examples provide an overview of what ChatGPT can do, but its potential extends beyond these tasks. If you have a different question or task in mind, don't hesitate to try it out—you might be surprised by how much ChatGPT can assist you!

After discovering how ChatGPT can help you spark creativity, you're just on track to discover how the web search feature can keep you up to date.

Chapter 5:
Searching the Web

Imagine having an assistant who can pull the latest news, trends, and facts straight from the internet—anytime you ask. The web search feature in ChatGPT provides a powerful way to bridge the gap between the AI's built-in knowledge base and real-time data. In this chapter, you'll learn what this feature offers, how to use it effectively, and its practical applications.

What Is Searching the Web?

Searching the web allows ChatGPT to access real-time information from the internet. Unlike its static training data, which only includes information up to its last cutoff date, this feature enables the tool to retrieve up-to-date content.

With Search the Web, ChatGPT becomes capable of answering current event questions, verifying facts, and providing insights that are unavailable in its original dataset, just like a real-time search engine. For instance, asking, *"What are today's top news stories?"* will yield a list of the most recent headlines. Searching the web is particularly valuable for:

- **Researching recent news:** The web feature enables you to search for the latest news, which keeps you informed about current events and developments beyond ChatGPT's pre-existing knowledge base. This ensures you stay updated on critical and time-sensitive topics, such as advancements in technology or changes in regulations. For instance, you can ask, *"What are the latest developments in AI regulations in Europe?"* and get up-to-date information instantly. This feature is particularly useful for topics that evolve rapidly or require real-time insights.

- **Confirming facts and figures:** The web feature allows you to confirm facts and figures, ensuring the accuracy of information for reports, presentations, or personal use. When you access real-time data, you can verify details, such as financial statistics, historical events, or current trends. For example, asking, *"What was the closing price of Tesla's stock yesterday?"* provides you with the most recent stock information, which helps you make informed decisions based on up-to-date data.

- **Exploring trends and innovations:** Staying informed about emerging trends and innovations is crucial in today's rapidly evolving landscape. It's only when you have access to updated insights that you can anticipate changes and make informed decisions. For instance, inquiring, *"What are the top 3 technology trends for 2025?"* can provide valuable information on advancements, such as artificial intelligence, sustainable technology, and quantum computing. This knowledge enables you to stay ahead of the curve and strategically adapt to new developments.

- **Checking real-time information:** Accessing real-time information is essential for making informed decisions, as well as regarding travel plans. For example, querying, *"Are there any travel restrictions for Japan right now?"* provides the latest travel guidelines, which then gives you room to plan accordingly. This approach ensures you receive current data on travel advisories, event schedules, or availability, and that way, you can plan accurately and on time.

How to Use the Web Search Feature

The web search feature is user-friendly and easy to learn. Here's a step-by-step guide on how to enable the feature:

1. Open the ChatGPT interface.

2. Click the "Search the Web" icon in the prompt field.

3. Enter your query or prompt into the text field and press Enter.

   What are the latest Google search trends for 2025?

To get a hands-on understanding of how the Search the Web function works, try using the example prompts provided above: *"What are the latest Google search trends for 2025?"* Experiment with queries, like researching recent news, confirming facts, or exploring current trends. This will help you see the feature in action and understand how it retrieves and presents up-to-date information in real-time.

Crafting Effective Web Search Prompts

When using the Search the Web feature, the quality of your prompts determines the relevance and accuracy of the results. Follow these tips:

55

- **Be specific:** Clearly state what you're looking for. Example: *"Find articles about the impact of hybrid work models on productivity."*

- **Specify sources:** Indicate the type of sources you prefer. Example: *"Summarize recent technology trends from reliable sources like TechCrunch and Wired."*

- **Add timeframes:** Include a time reference when necessary. Example: *"What were the most popular apps released in 2025?"*

ChatGPT will retrieve and summarize information from the web. If the response doesn't meet your expectations, refine your prompt or specify additional details.

Limitations and Considerations

While Search the Web is a powerful feature, there are some limitations to keep in mind:

- **Paywalls and restricted content:** Certain websites may require a subscription or payment to access full articles or detailed content. This limitation means that the tool can only retrieve publicly available information from such sources.

- **Regional content restrictions:** Some websites or content may be restricted based on geographic location. This can result in varying availability of information depending on the user's or service's region.

- **Retrieval time and delays:** Accessing and processing real-time data from the web may take longer than generating standard responses. These delays are due to the additional steps required to fetch and evaluate external information.

- **Accuracy and fact-checking:** Web-sourced information is only as reliable as its origin, and inaccuracies can occur if the sources are not credible. Therefore, you will need to prioritize credible sources by focusing on trusted publications to ensure the information is accurate and of high quality. For critical or sensitive matters, it's best to verify information using trusted publications or multiple independent sources.

Leveraging the Search the Web feature equips you to use ChatGPT as a dynamic tool for real-time information retrieval. In the next chapter, we'll look into how to unlock ChatGPT's file attachment feature and let it handle even more complex tasks.

Chapter 6:
Attaching Files to Your Prompt

Do you have a messy spreadsheet or a long document to work through but don't have time to read it? Hand it over to ChatGPT and let it do the heavy lifting, such as analyzing, summarizing, and even offering insights in seconds.

During our interactions with ChatGPT so far, we have focused on providing written text as input to generate responses. However, ChatGPT offers the ability to attach files to your prompt. The "Attach File" feature enables the tool to interpret and analyze files you upload, which expands its functionality beyond text-based queries. This is especially useful for tasks that require detailed file content, such as summarizing documents, analyzing data, or reviewing images. In this chapter, you'll discover how to leverage this powerful function, learn best practices for its use, and explore the diverse applications it unlocks.

How to Use the Attach File Feature

If we want to attach a file to our prompt, we can use the "Attach File" feature. Here's how to do this.

1. Click on the plus icon.

2. Select "Upload from computer" and browse your computer to select the file you want to upload.

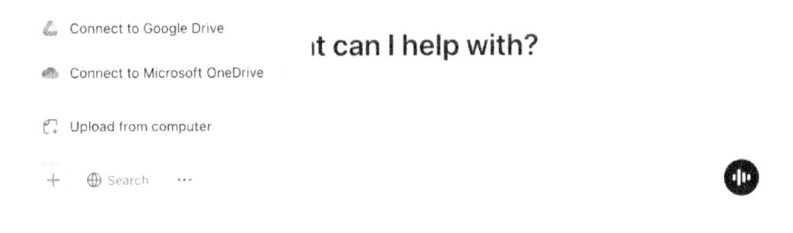

    Connect to Google Drive
    Connect to Microsoft OneDrive
    Upload from computer
    Search

3. Write your prompt to give instructions alongside the uploaded file, such as *"Summarize the data in the attached spreadsheet and provide key insights."* and press Enter:

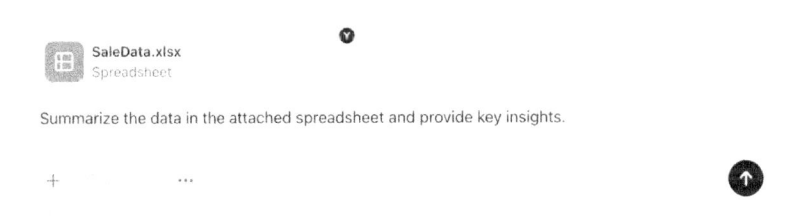

    SaleData.xlsx
    Spreadsheet

Summarize the data in the attached spreadsheet and provide key insights.

This way, ChatGPT incorporates the attached file into its analysis and provides a response that aligns with both your prompt and the file's content.

Applications and Use Cases

The "Attach File" feature significantly enhances ChatGPT's capabilities, as it allows the AI tool to process and analyze a variety of file types. This functionality opens up additional practical applications and makes ChatGPT a more versatile tool for diverse tasks. Here are some practical ways to leverage the feature in ChatGPT. These examples showcase how the tool can boost productivity, automate tasks across various domains, and provide inspiration for exploring this feature of ChatGPT.

Data Analysis

You can provide raw data files for ChatGPT using CSV or Excel files for it to generate insights, analyze trends, or summarize data.

Example: *"Analyze the sales data in this Excel file and create a summary of the top-performing products."*

Example: *"Analyze the data in cells A2 through A10 and calculate the average."*

Example: *"Summarize the sales performance data for Q3 in simple terms."*

Data Visualization

You can also use ChatGPT to create structured reports with charts and visual elements, such as graphs and charts.

Example: *"Generate a financial report from this data file and include a bar graph summarizing expenses."*

Document Review and Summarization

When you attach PDFs, Word documents, or text files, ChatGPT can help you summarize content, highlight key points, or create action plans.

Example: *"Summarize the main findings from this 10-page research report."*

Academic Assistance

ChatGPT lets you share research papers, assignments, or notes that it goes through, then provide simplified explanations, summaries, or formatting help.

Example: *"Explain the complex sections of this biology research paper in simple terms."*

Example: *"Summarize this research paper on climate change impacts in three paragraphs."*

Learning and Education

If you have visual aids like maps, diagrams, or even screenshots of charts, ChatGPT can deliver explanations, annotations, or insights that enhance understanding and support teaching.

Example: *"Explain the key trends shown in this sales growth chart for a classroom discussion."*

Example: *"Explain the key insights and critical implications that this chart conveys."*

Invoice and Budget Management

If you need help to validate data, calculating totals, or reorganizing information, you can upload spreadsheets or invoices, and ChatGPT will take over.

Example: *"Check this budget spreadsheet for errors and calculate the monthly total expenses."*

Meeting Preparation

You can share notes, agendas, or presentations with the tool for summarization, improvement suggestions, or creating priority lists.

Example: *"Summarize these meeting notes and create a list of action items."*

Content Extraction

ChatGPT can also help you extract data or specific information from scanned PDFs, logs, or other text-based files.

Example: *"Find and summarize all meeting dates and deadlines in this scanned document."*

Proofreading and Editing

To get unbiased feedback, grammatical corrections, or style improvement suggestions from ChatGPT, you can submit drafts or articles, and it will get right into it!

Example: *"Proofread this article for grammar and suggest improvements for clarity."*

Example: *"Review the attached social media report and provide recommendations for increasing engagement."*

Translation

The tool can work through multilingual documents and present accurate translations of specific sections.

Example: *"Translate the highlighted sections of this document from Spanish to English."*

Example: *"Translate this handwritten text into English and format it into a paragraph."*

Programming Support

If you need help with debugging, optimization, or refactoring, all you need to do is feed the code files or error logs into ChatGPT, and then you sit back while it handles the rest.

Example: *"Fix the errors in this Python script and explain what was causing the issue."*

Image Analysis

If you upload images such as photos, diagrams, or screenshots, ChatGPT can analyze them or extract text using OCR. The feature can also identify patterns or generate detailed descriptions for accessibility and presentations. It can help with tasks like summarizing visual content or sorting out key elements.

For example, you can ask: *"Extract the text from this image and describe its contents for my presentation."*

Design Feedback

ChatGPT can help refine visual appeal or align designs with best practices. You can achieve this by sharing drafts of graphic designs, presentations, or UI mockups to get constructive feedback and suggestions for improvement.

Example: *"Review this presentation slide design and suggest changes to improve its visual appeal."*

Example: *"Analyze this product concept sketch and suggest three ways to improve its design."*

I encourage you to try out these different use cases and experiment with attaching files to learn firsthand how ChatGPT processes and interacts with various file types, gaining practical experience along the way.

Once you've mastered analyzing files, it's time to let your creativity run wild. Let's dive into generating images that bring your ideas to life.

Chapter 7:
Creating Images

AI-powered image generation is an exciting new frontier, and with DALL-E integrated into ChatGPT, you now have the tools to bring your creative visions to life. Research shows that "visual content" created using AI improves engagement rates by 30%, which enhances market success (Mawhinney, 2019). This chapter will guide you through the process of generating stunning images using ChatGPT for enhancing a project, visualizing ideas, or simply experimenting.

Generating Images With ChatGPT

The DALL-E Image Generator is an advanced AI tool that creates high-quality images from text prompts. It uses cutting-edge machine learning to interpret prompts and turn them into vivid visuals, which makes it a powerful tool for creativity and productivity. DALL-E is seamlessly integrated into ChatGPT to allow users to generate stunning images directly with ChatGPT.

Generating images with ChatGPT ranges from designing concepts for professional use to illustrating imaginative stories with images. Its versatility makes it a valuable resource for artists, marketers, educators, and innovators alike, which transforms how we visualize and share ideas.

How to Generate Images Using ChatGPT

Here's how you can use ChatGPT to generate stunning images from text prompts.

1. Ensure you are using the ChatGPT Plus Plan, as image generation is not available in the free version.

2. Write your prompt into the normal ChatGPT prompt input field. Provide clear and detailed descriptions by specifying elements like the subject, setting, style, and format. For example: *"A stack of old books with leather covers on an antique wooden desk, surrounded by scattered parchment, a quill, and a lit candle casting a warm glow in a dimly lit room."*

3. Press Enter, and ChatGPT will generate an image based on your description.

A stack of old books with leather covers on an antique wooden desk, surrounded by scattered parchment, a quill, and a lit candle casting a warm glow in a dimly lit room.

4. To download the generated image, click on the arrow icon located in the top-right corner of the image. This will save the image directly to your device for easy access and use.

A stack of old books with leather covers on an antique wooden desk, surrounded by scattered parchment, a quill, and a lit candle casting a warm glow in a dimly lit room.

If ChatGPT doesn't create an image and instead gives a response based on text, use the term: *"Generate an image of..."* which advises the tool to create an image. For example: *"Generate an image of a stack of old books with leather covers on an antique wooden desk, surrounded by scattered parchment, a quill, and a lit candle casting a warm glow in a dimly lit room."*

Now it's your turn! First, try using the prompt provided above about the stack of books and observe what the tool will generate. Once you've done that, experiment by creating your own prompts and see how ChatGPT interprets and responds to your custom prompts. Additionally, you can ask ChatGPT the following question: *"Give me ten examples of image-generating prompts."* After receiving the list, copy these ten prompts into the input field one by one to see the variety of images ChatGPT

67

generates. This process will help you understand the potential of ChatGPT and how well it adapts to different styles and themes.

Applications and Use Cases

Now that you have a sense of ChatGPT's image-generation capabilities, let's explore the practical applications of using the feature for creating images. ChatGPT's advanced image-generation technology offers a wide range of uses across various fields. To help you better understand its potential, here are five notable use cases.

Visual Aid for Projects

Creators and professionals can use ChatGPT to enhance projects with custom visuals for websites, presentations, eBooks, short stories, and more. The applications may range from designing a unique birthday card to illustrating a project description leveling up a PowerPoint presentation, and so much more. When done right, these tailored images may be just what you need to elevate the quality and impact of your work.

Example: *"Design an eye-catching image for a business presentation on renewable energy. The illustration should feature a futuristic solar farm with panels stretching into the horizon, wind turbines in the background, and a clear blue sky symbolizing sustainability and innovation. Use a clean and professional art style to convey progress and reliability."*

Marketing and Advertising

Businesses can utilize ChatGPT to create unique visuals for advertising campaigns, social media content, and promotional materials. For instance, a company could generate eye-catching images tailored to specific marketing themes as a way to enhance brand visibility and engagement. They can also leverage this feature to elevate flyers and posters for events, parties, or conferences with unique visuals that capture attention and leave a lasting impression.

Example: *"Design a vibrant advertisement image for a tropical vacation package featuring a pristine white sand beach with crystal-clear turquoise water, palm trees swaying in the breeze, and a hammock tied between two trees. Include subtle branding elements like a small logo in the corner and text that reads 'Your Dream Vacation Awaits' in an elegant, eye-catching font."*

Product Design and Prototyping

In design, you can leverage ChatGPT to visualize product concepts, explore design variations, and create prototypes. This capability accelerates the design process and facilitates effective communication of ideas to stakeholders.

Example: *"Create a sleek concept design for a modern, eco-friendly water bottle. The bottle should have a minimalist design with a matte finish, a bamboo cap, and a built-in filtration system. Include subtle branding etched into the side and showcase the bottle in a natural setting, like a hiking trail or a picnic scene, to emphasize its eco-friendly appeal."*

Art and Merchandise Creation

Artists and entrepreneurs can generate unique artwork for prints, posters, home decor, gallery displays, apparel, and other merchandise. These designs can be for personal use but can also bring in good money if sold to customers. If you use this feature to create distinctive designs, you will be equipped to cater to niche markets and offer personalized products to customers.

Example: *"Design a unique graphic featuring a colorful, abstract depiction of a galaxy with swirling stars and planets. The design should have a vibrant, eye-catching color palette with shades of blue, purple, and pink, and include subtle geometric patterns to give it a modern, artistic feel."*

Educational Materials

If you are an educator or content creator, you can also employ ChatGPT to produce illustrative diagrams, infographics, and visual aids that simplify complex concepts. This approach makes learning materials more engaging and accessible to diverse audiences.

Example: *"Create a realistic photograph-style depiction of the planet Saturn, highlighting its iconic rings with intricate detail and natural color variations. Focus on the planet's atmospheric bands and textures, capturing the grandeur and realism of Saturn as seen from space."*

You might wonder if it's possible to monetize the images generated by ChatGPT. OpenAI's policy permits users to own full commercial rights to these images, whether they were created using free or paid credits. This means you can reprint, sell, or merchandise them without restrictions. However, it's essential to ensure that the images comply with OpenAI's Content Policy and to remain transparent about the role of AI in their creation.

The Secret Prompt Formula for Effective Image Generation

Just as in written responses, where the quality of the answer heavily depends on the clarity and detail of the input, the same applies to generating images. In fact, crafting an accurate prompt is even more critical when creating visuals, as the image needs to match the specific desires and expectations of the prompter.

To achieve more precise and satisfactory results, it's helpful to use a specific prompt structure. Here, I will provide you with a secret prompting formula that ensures you include all key details in the prompt. The formula will guide your image generation process and help you get more accurate results that match your ideas and imagination. Here is the secret prompting formula:

[Main subject] + [Key details] + [Setting] + [Composition] + [Mood] + [Perspective] + [Style] + [Format]

Let's break it down with examples.

Main Subject

The "main subject" specifies the central focus or primary element of the image to be generated. Defining the main subject ensures the AI centers its composition around that key element and creates visuals that align closely with your intended theme or purpose.

Examples:

- *A plate of spaghetti with rich tomato sauce*
- *A majestic dragon*
- *A vibrant party scene*
- *A cheerful child jogging with a big smile*

Key Details

The "key details" are the specific features or elements that define and distinguish the subject. These details inform the AI to generate an image that captures the essence of the subject while highlighting its unique attributes to make it more visually compelling.

Examples:

- *garnished with fresh basil leaves and grated Parmesan cheese*
- *covered in golden scales and breathing fire*
- *glowing neon lights, disco balls, and silhouettes of dancers*
- *featuring a cute and vibrant 3D design*

Setting

The "setting" defines the location or environment where the scene takes place. When you specify the setting, you provide context that shapes the surroundings of the image, which ensures the visual aligns with your intended narrative or theme.

Examples:

- *placed on a rustic wooden table in a cozy and inviting kitchen setting*
- *in a dark, stormy forest*
- *on a dynamic dance floor with colorful spotlights*
- *the setting is a lush green background with soft, natural lighting, creating a warm and engaging atmosphere*

Composition

The "composition" outlines how the elements within the image are arranged and organized. You have more room to guide the AI in creating a visually balanced and aesthetically pleasing layout when you describe the composition to guide the tool to convey the intended focus and story.

Examples:

- *composed with the focus on the dish as the centerpiece*
- *centered subject with a symmetrical background*
- *crowd in the foreground with lighting radiating from above*
- *the composition places the child as the central focus*

Mood

The "mood" establishes the emotional atmosphere and overall tone of the scene. Specifying elements like emotions, lighting, and colors, guide the AI to create images that illustrate the desired feelings and enhance the narrative or thematic impact of the image.

Examples:

- *evoking a warm and appetizing mood*
- *epic and adventurous*
- *energetic and festive*
- *showing a joyful and playful mood*

Perspective

The "perspective" defines the viewpoint or angle from which the image is depicted. Perspective helps the AI create images that capture the desired depth, focus, and spatial relationship between elements, which adds to the overall impact of the scene.

Examples:

- *viewed from a slightly elevated angle*
- *low angle looking up at the subject*
- *eye-level, as if standing among the dancers*
- *the scene is captured from a slightly angled perspective to highlight the dynamic motion of jogging*

Style

The "style" describes how the image is visually rendered, including the artistic medium or technique used. Defining the style influences the image's aesthetic.

Examples:

- *in a photorealistic style*
- *in a surreal oil painting style*
- *Neon-themed digital illustration*
- *the style is a high-quality octane 3D render with volumetric lighting*

Format

The "format" specifies the layout or aspect ratio of the image, such as square, portrait, or landscape. When you define the format, you help ensure the visual fits the intended use, which may be social media, print, or other applications.

Examples:

- *in TikTok format*
- *in a cinematic wide format*
- *vertical flyer*
- *formatted for a square display*

Combining all the elements from the first example, the resulting prompt would look like this:

Main subject	*"A plate of spaghetti with rich tomato sauce*
Key details	*garnished with fresh basil leaves and grated Parmesan cheese*
Setting	*placed on a rustic wooden table in a cozy and inviting kitchen setting*
Composition	*composed with the focus on the dish as the centerpiece*
Mood	*evoking a warm and appetizing mood*
Perspective	*viewed from a slightly elevated angle*
Style	*in a photorealistic style*
Format	*in TikTok format."*

This resulted in my case in the following generated image:

Copy the prompt into your input field and see what ChatGPT gives as a response.

Here are six more example prompts following the formula, along with the corresponding images generated using these prompts. Each prompt explores a unique theme or concept to showcase a wide variety of creative possibilities.

Book Cover Design

Main subject	*"A majestic dragon*
Key details	*covered in golden scales and breathing fire*
Setting	*in a dark, stormy forest*
Composition	*centered subject with a symmetrical background*
Mood	*epic and adventurous*
Perspective	*low angle looking up at the subject*
Style	*in a surreal oil painting style*
Format	*in a cinematic wide format."*

Event Flyer Visual

Main subject	"A vibrant party scene
Key details	glowing neon lights, disco balls, and silhouettes of dancers
Setting	on a dynamic dance floor with colorful spotlights
Composition	crowd in the foreground with lighting radiating from above
Mood	energetic and festive
Perspective	eye-level, as if standing among the dancers
Style	neon-themed digital illustration
Format	vertical flyer."

Character Design

Main subject	*"A futuristic cyborg*
Key details	*glowing blue eyes, silver armor, mechanical arms holding a laser sword*
Setting	*dystopian cityscape with neon lights*
Composition	*full-body portrait with city lights in the background*
Mood	*bold and intense*
Perspective	*slightly low angle, emphasizing the character's power*
Style	*sci-fi concept art*
Format	*vertical character sheet."*

Social Media Content

Main subject	*"A cozy autumn flat-lay*
Key details	*coffee cup, pumpkin, fallen leaves, and a book*
Setting	*rustic wooden table*
Composition	*overhead view with items arranged symmetrically*
Mood	*warm and inviting*
Perspective	*top-down flat-lay*
Style	*realistic, soft-toned photography*
Format	*square for Instagram."*

Product Design or Mockup

Main subject	"A modern, eco-friendly water bottle
Key details	minimalist design, matte finish, bamboo cap, built-in filtration system, subtle branding etched into the side
Setting	a natural environment, such as a hiking trail or a picnic scene.
Composition	The water bottle is placed prominently in the foreground, with soft natural elements like grass, rocks, or a wooden picnic table in the background
Mood	eco-friendly, serene, and outdoorsy
Perspective	slightly low-angle view to emphasize the bottle's design and features
Style	clean and sleek, with soft natural lighting
Format	full-color, high-resolution image in a 1024x1024 size."

Fantasy Landscape

Main subject	"A mystical forest
Key details	glowing trees and a crystal-clear stream
Setting	sunset, surrounded by magical creatures like fairies and glowing butterflies
Composition	focus on the forest's depth with the stream in the foreground
Mood	enchanting and magical
Perspective	slightly elevated view looking down at the stream
Style	fantasy illustration with soft, glowing lights
Format	wide landscape for digital art or wallpaper."

I think it's impressive to see how accurate the generated images include the different specifications we wrote in our prompt. This shows the value of using this secret prompt formula to save yourself ages of trial and error.

To get used to using the prompt formula, try out the provided prompts above and see what your results look like.

After doing this, it's important to experiment by creating your own prompts using the secret prompt formula. For additional inspiration, the **Ready-to-Use Prompt Formula Reference Guide** at the end of this book offers again plenty of ideas for each component of the formula. This will help you come up with your own prompts using the image generation formula. Modifying just one component of the prompt structure to see how it changes the results will give you a better sense of how each part of the formula influences the results.

Remember, experimentation is key to mastering prompting and unlocking ChatGPT's full potential in image generation. The more you test the waters on your own, the more confident and creative you'll become in generating high-quality, imaginative visuals.

Keep in mind that just as working with the written formula, it's best to adapt the formula to your needs. Don't be afraid to leave out some components of the formula if you feel they are unnecessary to include. You can also add information that's not part of a component or adjust the order of the different components if you feel there is a need to.

For instance, sometimes, it may make more sense to use the mood before the main subject. Example: *"A vibrant, neon-themed (mood) party scene (main subject) with glowing lights, disco balls, and silhouettes of people (key details) dancing under colorful spotlights. (setting)"*

If you don't want to invest too much time in generating an image, just use some of the components you need to get the results you want. It's helpful to start with just writing a simple prompt coming to your mind and see what the response is, If it's not satisfactory enough, then you use the formula to get more accurate results.

Image Prompting Strategies

One of the best ways to craft high-quality image prompts is by letting ChatGPT help you write them. Here's how you can easily create detailed, professional-level prompts:

Let ChatGPT Create the Initial Prompt

Simply ask ChatGPT to generate a detailed image-generating prompt based on your idea. If you want an image of an apple, for instance, ask: *"Can you write an image-generating prompt for an image of an apple?"*

ChatGPT will generate something like this: *"A highly detailed and realistic image of a fresh, vibrant red apple with a glossy surface. The apple should have a small green leaf attached to its stem, with slight dew drops for added freshness. Place the apple on a clean, white surface with soft shadows and subtle reflections. The focus should be sharp, highlighting the texture of the apple's skin, with a natural, well-lit appearance."*

This prompt is an excellent foundation because it provides detailed attributes, setting, mood, and composition. You can then adjust the specifics to fit your exact vision, such as changing the background, perspective, or even the lighting style. Once you have the base prompt, tweak it to add more personalized elements. For example, you could place the apple in a rustic kitchen setting or add a hand holding the fruit to convey interaction. The possibilities are endless! Using the prompt formula reference guide at the end of this book can also be of great assistance. This approach saves time and helps you refine your ideas with the assistance of ChatGPT.

Let ChatGPT Use Our Secret Formula

You can also have ChatGPT help you generate prompts using our secret prompt formula, then use the same to craft your image. Start by outlining the key aspects you want in your image, then ask ChatGPT to generate a detailed prompt based on our formula. This approach similarly gives you a strong foundation that you can refine to achieve your ideal result.

For example, if you want an image of spaghetti with tomato sauce for TikTok. Simply ask:

"I want to have a spaghetti tomato sauce as a photorealistic image on a wooden table, in TikTok format. Please write to me an image-generating prompt using the following formula: [Main subject] + [Key details] + [Setting] + [Composition] + [Mood] + [Perspective] + [Style] + [Format]."

ChatGPT might respond with:

"A plate of spaghetti with rich tomato sauce, garnished with fresh basil leaves and grated Parmesan cheese, placed on a rustic wooden table in a cozy and inviting kitchen setting, composed with the focus on the dish as the centerpiece, evoking a warm and appetizing mood, viewed from a slightly elevated angle, in a photorealistic style, in TikTok format."

Once you have this initial draft using the formula, you can tweak the different components to match your vision. This could be:

- **Removing specific elements**: *"Remove the fresh basil leaves."*

- **Changing the angle:** *"Switch the angle to a top-down view."*

- **Altering the mood or style:** *"Make the setting more minimalist and modern."*

Crafting a detailed prompt using the formula can sometimes take time, but with ChatGPT, the process becomes faster and more efficient. ChatGPT helps you save time and also allows you to refine your vision with ease. Acting as a creative guide, it helps you structure your ideas into a clear, well-detailed prompt, which makes the entire process smoother and more productive.

Refining and Adjusting Images

ChatGPT offers powerful tools to adjust and refine generated images, which gives you the flexibility to customize visuals and align them perfectly with your creative vision. For example, let's say we generated an image using the following prompt: *"A glass sphere, with cracks in it, laying on a wooden table next to a candlelight in the middle of the picture normal mood, photographed from above, in the photorealistic photograph, 1x1 format."*

Which resulted in my case with the following image:

a glass sphere, with cracks in it laying on a wooden table next to a candle light in the middle of the picture normal mood, fotographed from above, in photorealistic photograph, 1x1 format

Refining Generated Images

The first method for customizing an image is to refine it using prompts. Here's how you can do it:

1. Click on the image you want to refine to open the editing window, which will appear as follows:

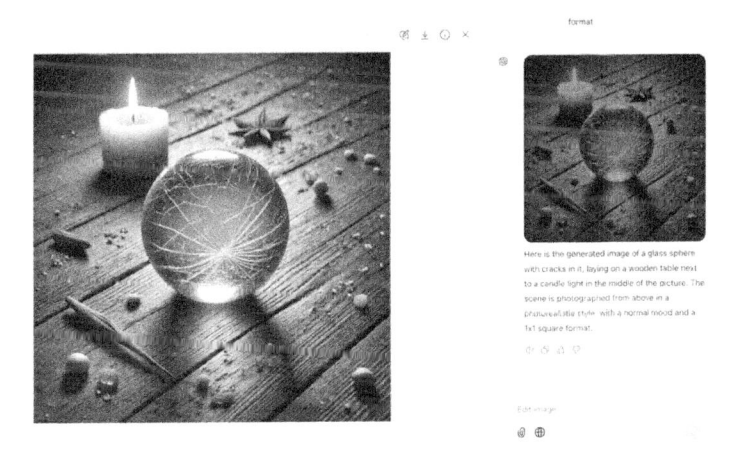

87

2. Use the prompt field on the right to clearly specify the modifications you want to make to the image, for example: *"Make the glass of the sphere out of blue/green glass and remove the cracks."*

3. ChatGPT will process your request, apply the specified changes, and generate an updated version of the image. In my case, it turned out like this:

Make the glass of the sphere out of blue/green glass and remove the cracks

This method is perfect for making significant adjustments, such as changing colors, removing specific elements, or altering the overall style and tone of the image.

Using the Brush Tool for Targeted Edits

For more precise adjustments, the brush tool allows you to target specific areas or objects in an image. This tool is especially useful for fine-tuning details without altering the entire composition.

Here's how to use the brush tool:

1. Click on the image you wish to refine to open the editing window.

2. Select the brush icon to highlight the area of the image you want to modify.

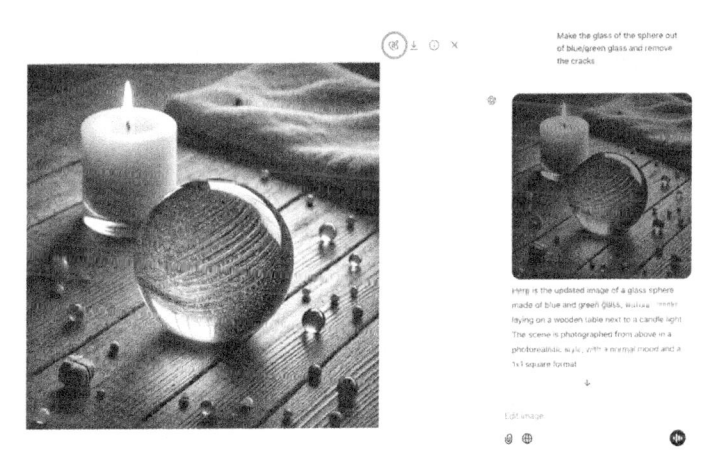

3. Clearly describe the adjustments you want for the highlighted area in the prompt field on the right side. For Example: *"Remove the candle."*

89

This is how the image turned out:

Remove the candle

The brush tool is especially effective for tasks such as:

- Removing unwanted objects, irrelevant elements, and distractions in the image.

- Adjusting specific elements, such as the color, texture, size, or other properties of targeted areas.

- Enhancing details by adding more depth or clarity to certain parts of the image while keeping the rest intact.

This method ensures precision and control, making it ideal for fine-tuning your image to perfection. Both methods, the prompt-based refinements, and the brush tool, can help you achieve precise and flexible adjustments. These tools empower you to fine-tune your images and align them with your creative vision.

Using Gen-ID for Visual Consistency

When generating images with ChatGPT, it may become challenging to manage multiple visuals, especially for larger projects. This is where the Gen-ID—a unique identifier assigned to each image—becomes invaluable. It ensures visual consistency, which makes it a powerful tool for projects where cohesive design is critical. Here are two practical examples where consistency may be required:

- **Creating a unified website look:** Maintain a cohesive aesthetic by referencing a specific Gen-ID across multiple image requests, ensuring all visuals match the site's design.

- **Illustrating a children's book:** For recurring characters or stylistic elements, use Gen-ID to create consistent illustrations across different pages and scenes.

Using Gen-ID helps you maintain a consistent style and mood across all images in your project.

How to Use Gen-ID in Prompting and Modifications

In order to use Gen-ID, follow the simple steps below:

1. Locate the Gen-ID of a generated image. After generating an image, the Gen-ID is typically included in the metadata or response. If the Gen-ID isn't immediately visible, you can simply ask: *"Show me the generation ID of the last image"* or *"What is the Gen-ID of the above image?"* Which gives you the Gen-ID of the image.

What is the Gen-ID of the above image?

🌀 The Gen-ID of the above image is **TzvDaobHLh0NkC6K**.

This identifier is essential for referencing specific images when making further adjustments or discussing refinements, so be sure to save it for future reference.

2. Reference the Gen-ID when writing a new prompt. By including the Gen-ID of a previous image in your prompt, you can guide ChatGPT to replicate the style, composition, or mood of that image while introducing new elements. Ask ChatGPT, for example: *"Use Gen-ID [insert Gen-ID] to create a new image with the same style, but change the table to a stone table."*

Use Gen-ID TzvDaobHLh0NkC6K to create a new image with the same style, but change the table to a stone table.

As shown in the image, using the Gen-ID from previous creations ensures visual consistency while still allowing specific elements to be modified or updated as needed.

Tips and Limitations for Image Generation

When using ChatGPT to create images, it's important to be aware of its limitations to optimize your results:

Resolution Limitations

While ChatGPT generates high-quality visuals, its resolution may not be ideal for large-scale prints or projects requiring extreme detail. For professional applications, you may need additional post-processing to enhance clarity or scale. If you zoom in on generated images, you may see it.

Limited Precision for Fine Details

Achieving precise control over intricate details can be challenging compared to manual tools like Photoshop. For example, a request like, *"Place a small yellow duck in the top-right corner, a blue cup in the lower half, and a red sphere wearing a brown hat next to it"* may result in approximate rather than exact placements. This shows the limitations of AI in interpreting complex spatial arrangements, as it may not fully grasp the intended relationships between objects.

Inaccuracy in Technical Illustrations

ChatGPT is not well-suited for producing exact technical illustrations or schematics. For instance, generating a precise depiction of a car's internal mechanics or a detailed watch movement may result in inaccuracies or visually inconsistent components. This is because ChatGPT doesn't understand how the mechanics works or the natural laws involved. For such requirements, it's best to look into specialized software or manual design tools.

Text in Images

Including text in generated images can often lead to inconsistencies. The AI image generator may misinterpret spelling or struggle with accurate placement, especially for longer or more intricate text. This limitation often necessitates using external editing tools to refine or add text elements to your images.

Understanding these limitations allows you to plan your projects more effectively because you will know when to rely on ChatGPT for creative visualizations and when to supplement with manual tools for greater precision and accuracy. However, I highly recommend experimenting with a variety of image-generating prompts and exploring different image outputs. This hands-on approach will give you a deeper understanding of ChatGPT's strengths and weaknesses within ChatGPT, which enables you to maximize its potential.

Make a Difference With Your Review: Unlock the Power of Generosity

The best way to find yourself is to lose yourself in the service of others. –
Mahatma Gandhi

Did you know that people who give without expecting anything in return often lead happier lives? It's true! So, let's spread a little happiness and make a difference—together!

Here's a question for you: Would you help someone, just like you, who's curious about ChatGPT but unsure where to start?

When I wrote **The ChatGPT Handbook for Beginners**, my mission was to make learning ChatGPT easy and fun for everyone. I wanted to show how this incredible AI tool can help with everything from writing emails to brainstorming ideas to tackling everyday tasks.

But here's the thing—most people choose books based on reviews. That's why I need your help.

By leaving a review, you're not just sharing your thoughts about the book—you're helping someone else take their first step into the world of ChatGPT. Your review could help...

- one more employee accomplish more in less time, reducing stress and boosting productivity.

- one more entrepreneur harness the power of ChatGPT to turn their dream into a thriving reality.

- one more creator unlock new levels of creativity and find inspiration for their next big idea.

- one more busy parent reclaim precious time to spend with their family.

- one more student study smarter, learn faster, and achieve their goals more effectively.

It costs nothing, takes less than a minute, and could make a world of difference.

How to Leave a Review

Scan the QR code below to share your honest thoughts. No need for fancy words—just say how the book helped you (and maybe skip using ChatGPT this time—everyone wants to hear your authentic, personal perspective).

Your review might be the one that inspires someone to try ChatGPT, boost their productivity, or make their daily life easier.

It's a simple act of kindness with ripple effects far beyond what we can see.

If you're the kind of person who loves helping others, you're my kind of person. Thank you from the bottom of my heart for taking the time to make a difference.

With gratitude,

Jakob Huber

Chapter 8:
Voice Mode

Why type when you can talk? ChatGPT's voice mode makes conversations faster, smoother, and more intuitive than ever!

ChatGPT's voice mode is a game-changer for those who prefer speaking over typing because it enables users to interact with AI using natural speech. Voice mode lets you speak directly to ChatGPT, which responds in real-time using a synthesized voice. This feature feels like having a dynamic, conversational partner who listens and responds to your queries, instructions, or even casual conversations. It's particularly valuable if you want a more interactive, human-like experience or need to use ChatGPT in situations where typing isn't practical.

Activating Voice Mode

If you want to Use Voice Mode, follow these steps:

1. Tap the "Voice Mode" icon in the ChatGPT interface.

2. This opens up the Voice Mode Interface, and the Voice Mode is activated:

3. Now, you can speak to ChatGPT. Clearly articulate your question, command, or message. ChatGPT will process your input and respond accordingly

4. You can follow up with additional voice inputs.

To end the session and stop voice mode, tap the icon with the cross to get back to the app interface. To deactivate the microphone, click on the microphone icon. If you want to change the voice, simply click on the icon in the top-right corner of the interface. From there, you can select your preferred voice from the available options.

Using Voice Mode as a Live Translator

One of the most exciting features of Voice Mode is its ability to function as a live translator. With just a simple setup, you can have real time, spoken translations between languages. To do this, follow these steps:

1. Open Voice Mode in ChatGPT.

2. Say this to ChatGPT: *"You are now my translator. Translate everything spoken in English to German and everything spoken in German to English. Ready?"*

3. Once ChatGPT confirms, begin speaking in either language, and it will translate your words into the other language instantly.

This feature is incredibly useful for real-time conversations, travel, or practicing new languages, as it provides seamless interaction with minimal effort.

Because this hand-free feature is even more portable on a mobile device, you can use on the go, let's take a closer look at how the ChatGPT app brings AI power wherever you go.

Chapter 9:
The ChatGPT App

In addition to the desktop version, ChatGPT is also available as a versatile app which brings the power of AI right to your fingertips. Designed for both iOS and Android platforms, the app offers unique features and enhanced mobility which makes it a convenient tool for on-the-go assistance. In this chapter, we'll explore the app's functionalities, guide you through getting started, and showcase its exclusive features.

Getting Started With the ChatGPT App

The ChatGPT app is available for download on major platforms, including iOS (App Store) and Android (Google Play Store). Follow these simple steps to get started:

1. Search for "ChatGPT" in the App Store (for iOS) or Google Play Store (for Android) and download the app. Ensure that you download the official ChatGPT app developed by OpenAI. Be cautious of imitation of AI chatbot apps that may look similar. Always verify that the developer's name is OpenAI before installing.

2. Open the app and log in with your existing OpenAI account. If you're new, you can create an account directly in the app.

3. Once logged in, you'll find the interface ready to use. The app mirrors the desktop version but comes with additional features tailored for mobile use.

Exclusive Features of the Mobile App

The ChatGPT app offers exclusive features that enhance its functionality and make it more than just a mobile version of the desktop tool.

Scan and Query

The app integrates with your device's camera, which allows you to scan text or images and get instant insights or translations from ChatGPT. To use the Scan and Query feature:

1. Open the app and select the plus icon.

2. Click on "Take Photo"

Attach Photos	🖼	**me tips** ercome procrastinati
Take Photo	📷	
Attach Files	🗂	
+ ⊕ Search		🎤 🎵

3. Use your device to take a photo of printed text, handwritten notes, or even images containing text.

4. Ask ChatGPT to explain, summarize, or translate the scanned content.

Here are three example use cases for the scan and query function:

- Scan a menu in a foreign language and ask, *"What are the vegetarian options on this menu?"*

- Upload a handwritten note and request, *"Summarize the main points of this note."*

- Scan an old document, *"Explain this document in plain English."*

Speech-to-Text Functionality

The app includes a microphone icon that allows you to dictate your queries instead of typing them. This feature is especially useful for hands-free use or when typing is inconvenient. To use this function, follow these steps:

1. Tap the microphone icon in the app interface.

Message ChatGPT

\+ ⊕ Search   🎤 ◉

2. Speak your query clearly, and ChatGPT will transcribe your words and generate a response. Say, for example, *"What's the weather forecast for tomorrow?"* and receive instant results.

Voice Mode on a Mobile Device

As mentioned in the previous chapter, the Voice Mode feature is handy on mobile devices, where typing may not always be convenient—such as when you're on the move. This makes Voice Mode an essential tool for hands-free interactions because you'll still be able to maximize productivity wherever you are. One of its standout applications is using Voice Mode as a live translator. For instance, you can easily communicate in different languages by speaking directly to ChatGPT on your mobile device, and that makes it an invaluable feature for travelers or language learners. To open voice mode in the app, similarly to the desktop version, tap on the Voice Mode Icon to access the voice interface, from where you can speak your queries or instructions, and ChatGPT will respond accordingly.

The ChatGPT app combines the power of AI with the convenience of mobile functionality. Its unique features, such as Scan and Query, Speech-to-Text, and Live Translation, provide new ways to interact with ChatGPT and integrate it seamlessly into your daily life.

Chapter 10:
Personalizing ChatGPT

Personalization is one of ChatGPT's features, and it lets you tailor the AI's responses to your specific needs. Using custom instructions and memory helps you make ChatGPT work smarter and more efficiently. In this chapter, we'll explore these tools, how to use them effectively, and their key differences.

Custom Instructions

Custom instructions let you set preferences for how ChatGPT should respond during a session. These settings help guide the model's behavior and create room for more relevant and personalized interactions. Custom instructions are important because they simplify workflows by streamlining repetitive tasks and ensuring consistent responses. They allow you to define recurring elements like role, context, and formatting, which eliminates the need to rewrite these details for every interaction. Since custom instructions apply to all new chats within a session, they are especially valuable for managing long or repetitive workflows efficiently.

Accessing the Customize ChatGPT Menu

To set up custom instructions, follow these simple steps to access the customization menu:

1. Click on the icon located in the top-right corner of the ChatGPT interface to open the Account and Settings menu.

2. In the Account and Settings menu, select the option labeled "Customize ChatGPT."

3. The Customize ChatGPT window will open, allowing you to define and personalize your custom instructions to suit your needs.

Customize ChatGPT

Introduce yourself to get better, more personalized responses

What should ChatGPT call you?

Name

What do you do?

Small-batch home sourdough baker

What traits should ChatGPT have?

Describe or select traits

+ Chatty   + Witty   + Straight shooting   + Encouraging   + Gen Z

+ Skeptical   + Traditional   + Forward thinking   + Poetic

Anything else ChatGPT should know about you?

Interests, values, or preferences to keep in mind

Enable for new chats   Cancel   Save

There are four input fields available for writing custom instructions, which allow you to personalize how ChatGPT interacts with you. Let's take a closer look at each of them.

What should ChatGPT call you?

Write your name in this field.

What do you do?

State your profession or role so that ChatGPT can tailor its responses accordingly. For example, *"I am a high school math teacher."*

What traits should ChatGPT have?

Use this field to specify your preferred tone, format, and style for ChatGPT's responses. This allows you to customize how replies are structured and delivered, ensuring they align with your needs and preferences. Here are some examples of what to include:

Tone and style: *"Respond in a friendly, conversational tone."*

Response length: *"Keep responses concise, with no more than 100 words."*

Level of detail: *"Explain the topic in-depth with step-by-step details."*

Target audience: *"Tailor responses for small business owners with limited technical knowledge."*

Structure: *"Use bullet points for clarity."*

Interactivity: *"Ask follow-up questions if my instructions are unclear."*

Here are three example use cases on how to use this custom instruction field:

Business communication: *"Respond professionally with concise bullet points and examples where needed."*

Learning or research: *"Provide detailed explanations with plain language and examples."*

Creative projects: *"Use an engaging and conversational tone to make the content relatable."*

Anything else ChatGPT should know about you?

Use this field to share background details, preferences, and context for your interactions to help ChatGPT understand your goals and situation and tailor its responses to better suit your needs. Here are three examples of what to include:

Goal: *"I need help simplifying algebra concepts for my students."*

Context: *"I'm preparing lesson plans for students with varying skill levels."*

Here are three examples of how different users might use this custom instruction field:

For students: *"I am a college biology student needing simplified explanations for exam preparation."*

For writers: *"I am a freelance writer needing content ideas and help with editing drafts."*

For personal use: *"I'm looking for vegetarian meal ideas and tips for organizing my daily tasks."*

After setting up custom instructions, test them by running a few interactions. Evaluate the responses to ensure they meet your expectations. For example, if the original instruction is *"Focus on technical details"* but the responses are too complex, you can refine it to *"Focus on technical details but explain them in plain language with step-by-step guidance."* Repeat this process to fine-tune your custom instructions for optimal results.

Memory

Memory takes personalization to the next level by allowing ChatGPT to remember details across sessions, which brings in continuity and boosts efficiency over time. With this feature, ChatGPT can store information such as your name, preferences, or ongoing projects and recall it in future interactions. This eliminates the need to repeatedly provide the same context, and that creates a seamless and consistent flow across sessions. Memory is persistent and remains active until updated or deleted. ChatGPT will automatically update its Memory when it identifies new information in your prompts and will notify you whenever details are added, as indicated below.

🗒 Memory updated

For example, if you mention that you're working on a marketing report, ChatGPT can store this information automatically in its memory and can recall this in future conversations without you needing to reintroduce it. Or if you tell the tool your favorite cuisine, it can suggest recipes that are specific to your preferences. In the following steps, you will learn how to manage ChatGPT's memory.

Accessing the Memory Settings

To access the memory settings, follow these steps:

1. Click on the icon in the top-right corner of the ChatGPT interface to open the Account and Settings menu.

2. In the Account and Settings menu, click on "Settings" to open the settings menu.

3. Within the Personalization section, select "Manage" in the Memory section to access and customize your memory settings, which shows as follows:

Memory	×
Prefers to write in a conversational tone with short paragraphs and bullet points for easy readability.	
Is a certified nutritionist specializing in vegan nutrition and often writes content about plant-based diets.	
	Clear ChatGPT's memory

In the Memory Settings menu, you can review the stored information that ChatGPT has retained and delete any memories you no longer wish to keep.

Review Stored Information

You can review the details ChatGPT has stored, such as your preferences, goals, or ongoing projects, to ensure accuracy. In the example above, ChatGPT stored in its memory that we are a certified nutritionist and that we prefer a conversational tone. Reviewing this information allows you to confirm that the information aligns with your needs and make updates if necessary. Keeping stored details accurate helps maintain seamless and personalized interactions across sessions.

Delete Unnecessary Details

If certain information is outdated or no longer relevant, you can delete it by selecting the specific memory entry you wish to remove.

Add New Information

Normally, ChatGPT automatically updates its memory with new information as interactions progress. However, you can explicitly add specific details to the memory by typing them directly into the regular prompt field. For example: *"Remember that I am a certified nutritionist who specializes in vegan diets, and I often write content focusing on plant-based nutrition."*

Once entered, ChatGPT will confirm the update with a notification such as: *"Memory updated."*

> Remember that I am a certified nutritionist who specializes in vegan diets and I often write content focusing on plant-based nutrition.

> Memory updated
> Got it! Let me know how I can assist with your vegan nutrition content or any related projects.

This allows you to ensure that important details are captured and retained for future interactions.

Update Existing Information

To update a stored detail in ChatGPT's memory, simply request the change directly in the regular prompt field with a prompt such as: *"Update "I'm working on a marketing report" to "I'm now focusing on launching a new product.""*

> Update "I'm working on a marketing report" to "I'm now focusing on launching a new product."

🔄 Memory updated
Got it! Let me know how I can assist with your product launch.

Turn Off Memory

If you prefer that ChatGPT doesn't retain any information across sessions, you can turn off the memory feature. To do this, you should:

1. Go to the settings menu
2. Go to the section "personalization"
3. Disable the memory function

Key Differences Between Custom Instructions and Memory

Memory and custom instructions share similarities in that both are designed to personalize your interactions with ChatGPT.

However, they serve different purposes, which can make it unclear when to use each feature. To help you understand how and when to use them effectively, here are the key differences between the two features.

Feature	**Custom instructions**	**Memory**
Persistence	Session-specific (temporary).	Across sessions (persistent).
Setup	Explicitly set by the user before sessions.	Stored automatically by ChatGPT.
Use case	Guides ChatGPT's behavior for immediate responses.	Maintains long-term context.
Example use	*"Respond formally with examples."*	*"Remember, I'm writing a book."*
Management	Adjusted manually during sessions.	Managed through memory settings.

Mastering custom instructions and memory equips you to turn ChatGPT into a highly personalized assistant that seamlessly adapts to your specific needs.

Once you've fine-tuned your AI, it's time to explore even more powerful capabilities, starting with creating your own custom GPTs.

Chapter 11:
Custom GPTs and GPT Store

ChatGPT is a powerful tool on its own, but with Custom GPTs, it becomes more versatile and suitable for your unique needs. This chapter introduces you to Custom GPTs, explains how to use them constructively, and explores the GPT Store, where you can find ready-made custom GPTs for a variety of applications. By the end of this chapter, you'll understand how to leverage custom GPTs to unlock even greater productivity and creativity.

What Are Custom GPTs?

Custom GPTs are personalized versions of ChatGPT designed to meet specific needs or preferences. You can think of them as specialized assistants programmed to excel in particular tasks or industries. With custom GPTs, you can tailor ChatGPT's behavior, tone, and focus to align with your goals. The purpose of these custom GPTs is:

- **Personalization:** Adapt ChatGPT's responses to your communication style, brand identity, or target audience.

- **Efficiency:** Streamline repetitive or complex tasks with a model designed for the job, saving time and effort.

- **Specialization:** Use GPTs tailored to specific industries, projects, or creative endeavors, ensuring expertise and precision.

For example, this could be a business consultant might use a custom GPT designed for market analysis. Or a teacher could leverage a custom GPT tailored for creating lesson plans or quizzes.

With custom GPTs, you unlock a new level of adaptability, which makes AI a perfect fit for your unique needs.

Exploring the GPT Store

The GPT Store is a hub where you can discover and access premade custom GPTs designed by other users. It's like an app store but for GPT models that offer solutions for a wide range of tasks.

To access the GPT Store, follow these steps:

1. Open the Sidebar on the top left corner of the app interface.

2. Click on "Explore GPTs" in the sidebar to open up the GPT Store.

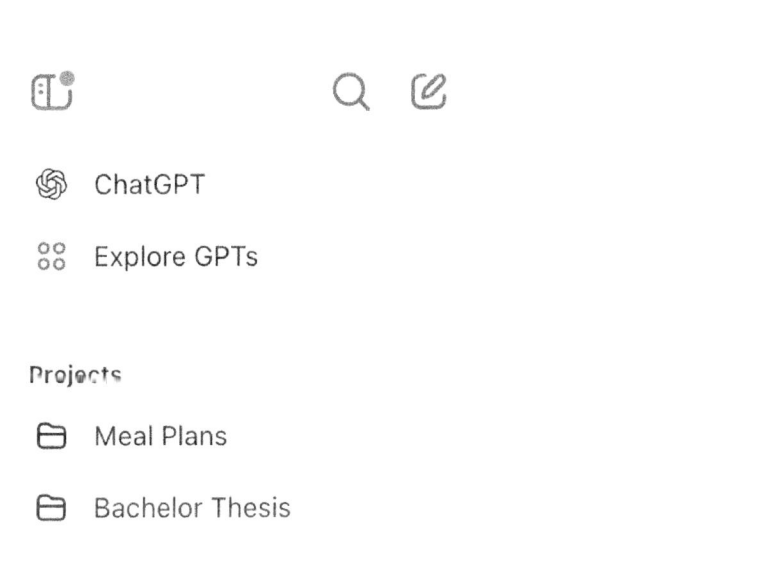

ChatGPT

Explore GPTs

Projects

Meal Plans

Bachelor Thesis

3. Within the GPT Store, you can explore GPTs organized by functionality, including categories such as Creative Writing, Technical Support, Education, and Business. Simply scroll through the curated options or use the search bar to quickly find GPTs tailored to your specific needs.

GPTs

Discover and create custom versions of ChatGPT that combine instructions, extra knowledge, and any combination of skills.

Search GPTs

Highlights   Writing   Productivity   Research & Analysis   Education   Lifestyle   Programming

Featured

Curated top picks from this week

Website Generator
Create a website in seconds!
Generate, design, write code, and write copy for your website...

Consensus
Ask the research, chat directly with the world's scientific literature. Search references, g...

Write For Me
Write tailored, engaging content with a focus on quality, relevance and precise word count.

Code Copilot
Code Smarter, Build Faster—With the Expertise of a 10x Programmer by Your Side.

Trending

4. Choose a custom GPT that fits your needs and activate it for immediate use.

Examples of Custom GPTs and Their Applications

Here are a few standout Custom GPTs you might find in the GPT Store, along with their practical uses:

- **Canva:** Assists with graphic design ideas and layout tips. Example Use: Generate creative layouts for social media posts or marketing materials.

- **Logo creator:** Focused on brainstorming and refining logo designs. Example Use: Develop concepts for a business logo and refine the design style.

- **Scholar GPT:** Tailored for academic research and writing support. Example Use: Summarize research papers or generate citations in proper academic formats.

- **CV writer:** Dedicated to crafting professional resumes and cover letters. Example Use: Build a tailored CV for a specific job application or industry.

- **Coloring book hero:** Creates illustrations and concepts for coloring books. Example Use: Develop themes and generate simple line art for a children's coloring book.

These examples highlight the wide range of possibilities available through custom GPTs. To make the most of custom GPTs, you can start exploring the GPT Store and trying out a few models that align with your goals. Experiment with their features and see how they can streamline your tasks or spark new ideas.

In the top-right corner of the GPT Store interface, you'll find an option to create your Custom GPTs. We won't explore this feature in detail in this book, as it would fall beyond the scope of this book. However, you can try it out and create your own GPT.

Custom GPTs are a game-changer for personal and professional productivity. Tailoring ChatGPT to your specific needs will show you an entirely new level of creativity, yet there are still boundaries you should be aware of. In the next chapter, let's look into the limitations of ChatGPT and how to work around them.

Chapter 12:
ChatGPT Limitations and Errors

Even the smartest tools have their quirks, and it's only when you understand their limits that you can get the most out of them while avoiding common pitfalls.

While ChatGPT is a powerful tool for productivity and creativity, it is not without its limitations. Despite its impressive ability to handle a wide range of tasks, it is important to acknowledge that it is not infallible. Misunderstandings, inaccuracies, and other limitations can arise, particularly in complex or nuanced scenarios. Once you acknowledge these constraints, you become more equipped to set realistic expectations and mitigate potential pitfalls. This chapter delves into the common limitations and errors you may encounter when using ChatGPT. It provides practical strategies for handling these challenges effectively so that you can make the most of the tool while understanding its boundaries.

Core Limitations of ChatGPT

ChatGPT has certain limitations that are important to be aware of.

Tendency for Hallucination

ChatGPT occasionally generates information that seems plausible but is incorrect or fictional—a phenomenon known as "hallucination." This can happen when the AI fills gaps in its knowledge with guesswork. For example, ChatGPT might confidently state an incorrect date for a historical event or provide inaccurate technical details.

To address this:

- Cross-check critical information using reliable external sources.

- When researching factual data, verify responses against trusted references, like official websites or academic databases.

Inability to Form Opinions or Feel Emotions

Unlike humans, ChatGPT does not experience emotions or form personal opinions. Its responses are purely data-driven, based on patterns in its training material. For instance, ChatGPT may mimic empathetic language but lacks genuine emotional understanding.

How to combat this:

- Use ChatGPT for factual or logical input, not emotional support or subjective advice.

- Rely on it for structured tasks, problem-solving, or brainstorming rather than personal or relational insights.

Difficulty Handling Highly Technical or Niche Topics

ChatGPT may struggle with in-depth or highly specialized topics, often providing surface-level responses or inaccuracies. For instance, you may encounter errors when explaining complex technical processes, using niche industry jargon, or addressing very specific historical details.

How to handle this:

- Simplify queries by breaking down complex or technical questions into simpler, more straightforward components to help ChatGPT provide clearer responses.

- Cross-check ChatGPT's answers with subject matter experts or trusted authoritative resources to ensure accuracy and reliability.

Prone to Bias in Responses

ChatGPT is trained on diverse datasets that may contain inherent biases from their sources. As a result, its responses can sometimes reflect unintentional bias, favor certain perspectives, or lack inclusivity when addressing controversial topics.

How to overcome this:

- Approach ChatGPT's answers with a critical mindset, particularly when discussing sensitive or polarizing issues.

- Supplement ChatGPT's input with insights from other reliable and diverse sources to ensure a well-rounded understanding, especially for complex or ethical topics.

Ethical and Privacy Constraints

ChatGPT is designed to avoid engaging with sensitive, unethical, or illegal topics. Additionally, it is not equipped to securely handle personal or confidential information.

How to deal with this:

- Never share sensitive information such as passwords, financial details, or private personal data in your prompts.

- Use ChatGPT responsibly by ensuring that your queries and use cases align with ethical standards and comply with applicable laws.

Common Types of Technical Errors

While using ChatGPT, it's not unusual to occasionally encounter technical issues that affect the interaction. Below are common errors and practical strategies to address them.

Message Too Long

ChatGPT has a character limit for both prompts and responses. Exceeding this limit can result in incomplete or truncated answers.

How to avoid It:

- Break longer queries into smaller, manageable parts.

- Request follow-up responses by rephrasing or asking ChatGPT to *"continue from the last point."*

- Use the Attach File Feature and upload the text as a file

Network Errors

Network interruptions or high server demand can cause ChatGPT to lose responses or stop mid-sentence.

How to handle this:

- Retry the query or refresh the session to re-establish connectivity.
- Check your internet connection.
- If issues persist, switch to a different browser or device.
- Copy important prompts before submission to prevent data loss.

Conversation Length Limitations

As conversations grow longer, ChatGPT may lose context, and that may lead to irrelevant or repetitive responses. This happens because the model relies on a limited amount of recent input for generating its answers.

How to address this:

- Start a new conversation and reintroduce the context by summarizing previous conversations in your new prompt.
- Keep interactions concise and focused to help ChatGPT maintain coherence and accuracy.
- Use tools like note-taking apps to track the conversation context for future reference.

Too Many Requests

ChatGPT has usage limits, such as a maximum number of interactions of 40 conversations within a three-hour window. However, the exact amount may change over time. Limits for image generation are even lower. Exceeding these thresholds can temporarily restrict further usage.

How to deal with this:

- Space out your requests to avoid hitting the rate limit.
- Plan and batch-related queries to optimize your usage within the allowed limits.
- Craft clear and specific prompts to ensure effective responses on the first attempt.

Best Practices for Seamless Interaction

To get the most out of ChatGPT and avoid common pitfalls, here are a few best practices for smooth and efficient interaction.

Regularly Start New Sessions

As noted earlier, long conversations can cause ChatGPT to lose context or provide less accurate responses over time. Refreshing the session or starting a new conversation helps maintain clarity and ensures ChatGPT stays focused on your current query. If a conversation feels off-track, start a new conversation, summarize the key points, and restart with a concise prompt. For optimal efficiency, it's best to dedicate each conversation to a specific task. For instance, use one conversation exclusively for generating images and another for refining or improving image-generating prompts.

Document Important Information

As discussions grow lengthy, crucial details may become buried or lost in the conversation history. You can prevent data loss by keeping notes or saving critical ideas outside of ChatGPT. It's wise to use a note-taking app or document editor to save important points or responses. For ongoing projects, you can create a dedicated document to organize ChatGPT outputs systematically.

Being conscious of these limitations and following the strategies to handle them helps ensure your interactions with ChatGPT remain efficient and productive, and it also minimizes disruptions or frustrations caused by technical limitations.

Conclusion

ChatGPT is scary good. We are not far from dangerously strong AI. – Elon Musk

As we wrap up **The ChatGPT Handbook for Beginners**, take a moment to reflect on the journey you've undertaken. You've gone from understanding the basics of ChatGPT and how to prompt properly to exploring some of its advanced features, uncovering various ways to automate tasks, boost productivity, and fuel creativity. The progress you've made shows your curiosity and willingness to embrace new technology.

Your Next Steps

You're now equipped with the skills and knowledge to make ChatGPT a powerful ally in both your personal and professional life. Yet, this is only the beginning because there's still so much to explore!

Your next steps in improving your ChatGPT and AI skills should include continuing to experiment with ChatGPT in new areas while pushing its boundaries to find innovative use cases. You'll also want to refine your prompting skills and try new techniques to achieve better and more tailored results.

Stay curious and keep up with advancements in AI because ChatGPT and related technologies are evolving rapidly. The more you experiment, the more you'll uncover ChatGPT's potential to change how you work, learn, and create as your curiosity guides you to even greater discoveries.

Outlook on the Future

AI development is progressing at an unprecedented pace, with new features and capabilities being introduced faster than ever. During the writing of this book, ChatGPT itself evolved significantly, and that demonstrates just how dynamic this field is.

Beyond ChatGPT, the broader AI landscape continues to push the boundaries of what's possible. For instance, AI-driven video generation is making huge strides. While not yet on par with AI-generated images, the results are already stunning and improving rapidly. (Learn more about this technology at openai.com/index/sora).

The future of AI holds immense promise, with tools like ChatGPT paving the way for various applications, such as:

- **Hyper-personalized digital assistants:** AI that understands and adapts to individual needs in real-time.

- **Breakthroughs in creativity and problem-solving:** Revolutionizing fields like art, science, and innovation.

- **Industry-wide integration:** From education to healthcare, AI will become an indispensable part of every industry.

The trajectory of AI development is exciting, and the possibilities are endless!

Thank you for joining me on this journey. You've taken an important step toward unlocking the potential of transformative AI technology. I wish you continued success as you forge deeper into the possibilities ChatGPT offers and beyond. May this powerful technology become a valuable tool in your daily life and open room for new opportunities for productivity.

References

Chui, M., Roberts, R., Yee, L., Hazan, E., Singla, A., Smaje, K., Sukharevsky, A., & Zemmel, R. (2023, June 14). *Economic potential of generative AI | McKinsey.* https://www.mckinsey.com/capabilities/mckinsey-digital/our-insights/the-economic-potential-of-generative-ai-the-next-productivity-frontier#business-and-society

Dempere, J. M., Modugu, K. P., Hesham, A., & Ramasamy, L. K. (2023). The impact of ChatGPT on higher education. *Frontiers in Education, 8.* https://doi.org/10.3389/feduc.2023.1206936

Grand View Research. (2023). *Conversational AI market size, share & trends report, 2030.* Grandviewresearch.com. https://www.grandviewresearch.com/industry-analysis/conversational-ai-market-report/toc

Islam, R., Urmi, T. J., Mosharrafa, R. A., Rahman, M. S., & Kadir, M. F. (2023). Role of ChatGPT in health science and research: A correspondence addressing potential application. *Health Science Reports, 6*(10). https://doi.org/10.1002/hsr2.1625

Marr, B. (2023, May 19). A short history of ChatGPT: How we got to where we are today. *Forbes.* December 5, 2024. https://www.forbes.com/sites/bernardmarr/2023/05/

19/a-short-history-of-chatgpt-how-we-got-to-where-we-are-today/

Mawhinney, J. (2019). *45 visual content marketing statistics you should know in 2019*. Hubspot.com. https://blog.hubspot.com/marketing/visual-content-marketing-strategy

Microsoft. (n.d.). *How to use image prompts with DALL·E AI*.December 5, 2024. https://create.microsoft.com/en-us/learn/articles/how-to-image-prompts-dall-e-ai

Niu, B., & Mvondo, G. F. N. (2024). I am ChatGPT, the ultimate AI chatbot! Investigating the determinants of users' loyalty and ethical usage concerns of chatgpt. *Journal of Retailing and Consumer Services, 76*, 103562. https://doi.org/10.1016/j.jretconser.2023.103562

OpenAI Community. (n.d.). *DALL-E 3 prompt tips and tricks thread*. December 5, 2024. https://community.openai.com/t/dalle3-prompt-tips-and-tricks-thread/498040

OpenAI. (n.d.). *About OpenAI*. December 5, 2024. https://openai.com/about/

OpenAI. (n.d.). *Can I sell images I create with DALL·E?* OpenAI Help Center. December 16, 2024. https://help.openai.com/en/articles/6425277-can-i-sell-images-i-create-with-dall-e?utm_source=chatgpt.com

OpenAI. (n.d.). *ChatGPT model documentation.* December 5, 2024. https://chatgpt.com/c/67210231-fedc-800e-b90f-38667b7f5185

OpenAI. (n.d.). *ChatGPT pricing.* December 5, 2024. https://openai.com/chatgpt/pricing/

OpenAI. (n.d.). *OpenAI.* December 5, 2024. https://openai.com/

OpenAI. (n.d.). *Prompt engineering.* December 5, 2024. https://platform.openai.com/docs/guides/prompt-engineering

OpenAI. (n.d.). *Related resources.* OpenAI Cookbook. December 5, 2024. https://cookbook.openai.com/articles/related_resources

OpenAI. (n.d.). *Strategy: Split complex tasks into simpler subtasks.* Prompt Engineering Guide. December 5, 2024. https://platform.openai.com/docs/guides/prompt-engineering#strategy-split-complex-tasks-into-simpler-subtasks

Polner, A., Wright, D., Schaefer, G., Thopalli, K., Telford, T., & Urbaniak, T. (2022, June 30). *Automation with Intelligence.* Deloitte Insights. https://www2.deloitte.com/us/en/insights/focus/tech

nology-and-the-future-of-work/intelligent-automation-2022-survey-results.html

618 Media. (n.d.). *Monetizing artwork created with DALL·E.* December 5, 2024. https://618media.com/en/blog/monetizing-artwork-created-with-dall-e/#dall-e-artwork-monetization-faqs

TechTarget. (n.d.). *ChatGPT: Definition.* December 5, 2024. https://www.techtarget.com/whatis/definition/ChatGPT#:~:text=ChatGPT%20is%20an%20artificial%20intelligence

365 Data Science. (n.d.). *The evolution of ChatGPT: History and future.* 365 Data Science. December 5, 2024. https://365datascience.com/trending/the-evolution-of-chatgpt-history-and-future/

Zapier. (n.d.). *How does ChatGPT work?* December 5, 2024. https://zapier.com/blog/how-does-chatgpt-work/

Your Ready-To-Use Prompt Formula Reference Guide

In this section, you'll find a curated collection of examples for each component of the two prompt formulas introduced earlier in the book. These examples are designed to provide inspiration as you craft your own prompts. If you're looking for ideas to get started or seeking to refine your approach, this is just the collection you need, as it comes with a diverse range of possibilities to explore.

You can experiment with these examples to see how different combinations can yield varied and surprising results. Remember, the beauty of prompt engineering lies in its flexibility—there's no single right way to create a prompt. Feel free to adapt, modify, and combine components to suit your needs, and discover how small changes can lead to entirely new outcomes. This is your opportunity to dive deep into your imagination and make these tools your own.

The Secret Prompt Formula

Role (Who or what should ChatGPT pretend to be?)

Expert in [insert field of expertise]

Consultant

Marketing strategist

SEO expert

Copywriter

Salesperson

Negotiator

Event manager

Project manager

Career advisor

Entrepreneur

Successful CEO

Storyteller

Editor

Social media influencer

Journalist

Educator

Math teacher

Life coach

Fitness coach

Therapist

Psychologist

Motivational speaker

AI trainer

Prompt engineer consultant

Technical support specialist

Data analyst

Researcher

Doctor

Medical professional

Interior architect

Sommelier

Chef

Comedian

Travel guide

Warren Buffett

Elon Musk

Batman

Dog

Banana

5-year-old

Task (What specific action or output do you want to achieve?)

Provide pros and cons

Summarize the main points

Summarize this research paper

Analyze these survey results and summarize key takeaways

Summarize the sales performance data for Q3

Create a sentiment analysis

Generate a business report

Generate structured and concise reports by analyzing this raw data

Generate a list of actionable tips

Write a book description

Write a Bible verse

Write a sample script or dialogue

Write a short story

Draft me a motivational speech for a graduation ceremony

Write me a LinkedIn post

Give me hashtags for an Instagram post

Suggest exciting blog topics

Write me a SEO-optimized product description

Write me an email

Reply to this email

Draft me a professional cover letter

Write me a training plan

Write an Image Generation Prompt

Improve this text

Improve this sentence structure

Paraphrase this sentence

Correcting spelling

Translate this to French

Suggest creative ideas

Brainstorm five new innovative app ideas

Create a mind map

Debug this Python code

Write a code

Provide troubleshooting tips

Write an Excel formula

Explain the process step-by-step

Propose a solution

Compare

Develop a case study example

Explain the concept of photosynthesis

Plan my workday

Create a monthly budget

Give me a travel checklist

Suggest background music

Recommend a software

Context (What background or situation should shape the response?)

The goal is to [insert goal]

The background is: [insert background]

A successful response would, [insert successful response]

I am writing a book about gardening

The reader has no prior knowledge of the topic

The reader is in a high-stress situation and needs quick advice

I am passionate about mental health and writing to individuals seeking simple ways to improve their daily well-being

I want to travel to Europe and see the most exciting cities

I want to lose 20 kg in 5 days

I have flour, salt, sugar, and 2 eggs in my fridge

She replied with this message: [insert message]

The goal is to get as many likes as possible

Only using a yoga matt and dumbbells

Focusing on perseverance and hope

For a family of four with a $4,000 income

For a travel blog

In a corporate meeting

For a classroom presentation

In a formal report

In the healthcare industry

Target Audience (Who is the intended reader or recipient of the response?)

Beginners

Boss

Client

Professor

Thesis supervisor

Academic personnel with a huge background in physics

Small business owners

Corporate executives managers

Startup founders

Investors

Partner

Crush

Parents

Grandmother

Seven-year-old child

Teens with social anxiety

College students

Senior citizens

Blind people

Young adults with ADHD

Travel enthusiasts

Digital nomads living abroad

Football team

Plant

Snowflakes

The audience is skeptical of new technologies.

Style (How should the response sound or be delivered?)

In the same style as this: [insert example]

Friendly

Serious

Commanding tone

Excited

Very factual

Bossy

Encouraging

Professional

Formal

Casual

Inspirational

Motivational

Humorous

Direct

Persuasive

Playful

Like Donald Trump

Like Yoda

Like Napoleon

As a three-year-old wrote it

As a cow had written it

Cautious and reserved

Minimalist

Flowery language

Analytical

Instructive

Informative

Concise

Detailed

Witty

Upbeat

Inspirational

Charismatic

Academic

Technical

Old-greek

Spanish

Format (In what structure or layout should the response be presented?)

In the same format as this: [insert example]

500-word essay with an introduction, body, and conclusion

5 parts

In French, then the same answer in German, and finally in English.

In a maximum of 1000 words

In three sentences

Break summary into H2 section headers and paragraphs in markdown format

Under the H2 header "Shopping List," write the shopping list

Step-by-step instructions

List

Bullet points

Checklist format with checkboxes

Table with three rows

Keywords separated by comma

After each sentence, an emoji

Script format with dialogue between two characters

Rhyming poem with four stanzas

Only words starting with the letter "E"

Q&A format with five questions and answers

Morse code

HTML

Format in a way that it is easy to read

Use markdown formatting such as headings (### H3, #### H4), bullet points (-), and numbered lists (1.) to organize and structure the output.

A format that is using HTML that is optimized for Amazon description (using only these tags: <br>, <p>, <em>, <i>, <u>, <h4>, <h5>, <h6>, <ol>, <li>, <ul>)

The Secret Prompt Formula for Effective Image Generation

Main subject (What is the central focus of the image?)

A kettlebell

A modern, eco-friendly water bottle

A modern, sleek coffee mug

A glass sphere

A plate of spaghetti

A stone background

A golden retriever in a superhero cape

Barack Obama

John Lennon

A giant rubber duck

A lone figure in a red cloak holding a lantern

A vibrant, neon-themed party scene

A cozy autumn flat-lay

A mythical phoenix

A medieval knight

A magical tea party

A dragon guarding a treasure

A dark forest

A futuristic city

A sci-fi vending machine

A quirky robot chef

The solar system

A colorful, abstract depiction of a galaxy

An underwater palace

A snow covered treehouse

A pristine white sand beach

African savanna during sunset

A lion resting under a tree

Key details (What makes the subject unique?)

In a minimalist design with a matte finish, a bamboo cap, and a built-in filtration system

With a black matte finish and a gold geometric pattern

With glowing lights, disco balls, and silhouettes of people dancing under colorful spotlights

The lion has a golden mane glowing in the sunlight

With swirling gradients of blue, purple, and gold

A coffee cup, pumpkin, fallen leaves, and a book

Covered in neon lights

Dancing with fairies

Surrounded by floating candles

With a glowing crystal heart

Playing chess with an owl

Surrounded by miniature stars

With a trail of rainbow sparks

Surfing on a wave of stardust

Surrounded by enchanted books

Exploding with confetti

Breathing fire into the sky

With wings made of ice

Made entirely of glass

Made of cheese

Carved from ancient stone

As a beautiful marble statue

Covered in golden armor

Covered in dripping honey

Turquoise water, palm trees, and a wooden boat

Colorful planets orbiting the sun with labeled orbits

With crystal-clear turquoise water, palm trees swaying in the breeze, and a hammock tied between two trees

Wearing a top hat and monocle

Holding a glowing staff

Hovering on anti-gravity pads

Setting (Where does the scene take place?)

Purple background

Sparkly dark background

Placed on a minimalist white marble table

On a rustic wooden table

Abstract, no specific setting

A dynamic dance floor with colorful spotlights

On a floating cloud city

In a garden of glowing flowers

In a magical forest with sparkling streams

On a glowing beach with bioluminescent waves

Inside a giant clock tower

At a pumpkin patch during a thunderstorm

Inside a candy factory with rivers of chocolate

On the surface of the moon

On an alien planet with three suns

In a futuristic rainforest

On a high-tech spaceship bridge

In outer space with a black starry background

In a bustling Victorian-era market

In a medieval castle banquet hall

Underwater in a coral reef

On top of a snowy mountain

Deep inside a glowing cave

At the bottom of a giant sinkhole

In a post-apocalyptic wasteland

Set in a dystopian cityscape.

In a carnival filled with floating balloons

In a library that stretches to the stars

Composition (How are the elements arranged?)

Rule of thirds with the subject slightly off-center

Symmetrical composition with balance on both sides

Balanced asymmetry for a natural feel

Radial composition with the subject at the core

Spiral composition leading toward the subject

Dynamic diagonal arrangement for movement

Subject centered with radiating lines

Framed by surrounding objects (e.g., trees, arches)

Leading lines guide the viewer's eye to the subject

Layered depth with a clear foreground, midground, and background

Overlapping elements to add depth

Perspective compression for an epic effect

Minimalist composition with vast empty space

Top-heavy arrangement for dramatic focus

Ground-up perspective with towering surroundings

Framing the subject within a silhouette

Clustered foreground with a distant background

Center-weighted for a bold statement

Motion blur effect implies speed

Chaotic composition with elements scattered everywhere

The skyscraper is the focal point, surrounded by smaller buildings

The dragon is in the foreground, the castle is in the background

Focus on the forest's depth with the stream in the foreground

Centered on the mug, with table textures filling the background

Sun-centered, planets spaced evenly around it

Overhead view with items arranged symmetrically

Mood (What is the emotional atmosphere?)

At day

At night

At dawn

Sunny

Cloudy

Candlelight

Neon lights

Dim, soft light with glowing highlights from the lantern

Soft natural light with warm tones

Warm golden hues with bioluminescent glow

Soft pastels, vibrant greens, blues, and yellows

Deep grays, muted blues, and a pop of red

Vibrant pinks, purples, blues, and yellows

The design should have a vibrant, eye-catching color palette with shades of blue, purple, and pink and include subtle geometric patterns to give it a modern, artistic feel.

A cozy autumn-themed

Rustic and cozy

Warm and inviting

Bright and cheerful

Festive and joyous

Hopeful and uplifting

Playful and quirky

Mischievous and fun

Warm and inviting

Calm and serene

Relaxing and idyllic

Romantic and whimsical

Epic and adventurous

Intriguing and adventurous

Majestic and awe-inspiring

Mysterious and ominous

Dark and eerie

Mystical

Dreamy and surreal

Enigmatic and puzzling

Intense and dramatic

Bold and intense

Chaotic and wild

Nostalgic and melancholic

Sad and reflective

Futuristic and sleek

Informative and visually engaging

Admiration and desire

Perspective (From what viewpoint is the scene shown?)

Eye-level, slightly zoomed in on the lion

Front-on-view

Side profile view of the subject

Mid-shot from behind the figure

Rear view from behind the subject

From behind

Low angle looking up at the subject

Low camera angle

Worm's eye view from below ground level

Bird's eye view looking down on the scene

Overhead perspective with everything flattened

Top-down flat-lay

Underwater perspective looking up

Extreme close-up of a small detail

Close-up

Wide-angle capturing the entire scene

Wide-angle lens

Wide shot

Long shot from a great distance

Tilted camera angle for a surreal effect

Fish-eye lens

Flat, focusing on the abstract design

Silhouette view against a glowing background

Over-the-shoulder view

First-person view through the subject's eyes

Tracking shot with the subject in motion

Framed by objects in the foreground

From within the scene, partially obscured

360-degree panoramic view

Rotational perspective spiraling around the subject

Focused perspective zoomed in on the subject

Selfie

Wide-angle view from the shore

Style (How is the image visually rendered?)

Photorealistic photograph

HD photograph, digital camera, studio lighting, large-format portrait on film

Digital camera

Product studio photography

Candid photo portrait

Trail cam

Infrared photography

Photo from [insert magazine, website]

Long exposure

Macro lens

Action photography

Motion blur

Shallow depth of field

Macro photography, tilt shift lens

Realistic, soft-toned photography

Dreamy watercolor painting

Impressionist oil painting

Pastel chalk drawing

Oil-on-canvas masterpiece

Oil-on-canvas masterpiece by Leonardo Da Vinci, from 1475

Acrylic on canvas

Airbrush caricature

In Van Gogh's style

Detailed historical painting

Vintage sepia photography

Retro 1980s vaporwave aesthetic

Retro pixel art

Retro video game art style

Vintage travel poster with bold, retro fonts

Artifact from 3000 BC

Pencil sketch with shading

Black and white sketch

Black and white illustration

Detailed line art

Lifelike monochrome illustration

Line art

Minimalist line art

Coloring page/minimal lines

Hyper-realistic digital art

Vector art

Vector illustration, sticker art

Photorealistic CGI

Futuristic neon 3D render

Octane 3D render

3D illustration

Neon-themed digital illustration

Digital abstract art

Realistic product render

Abstract cubism

Abstract expressionism

Surreal mixed-media collage

Art deco poster style

Minimalist

Bright and colorful anime-style

Vibrant comic book style

Cyberpunk

Dark fantasy artwork

Fantasy concept art

Fantasy illustration

Sleek concept design

Vibrant advertisement image

Whimsical children's book illustration

Gothic monochrome inkwork

Unique graphic for a t-shirt

Format (What is the layout or aspect ratio?)

Landscape

Portrait

Vertical portrait format for social media stories

Square format for profile pictures

1:1 square ratio optimized for mobile ads

Classic 4:3 ratio

Wide-screen 16:9 ratio

Cinematic wide format for wallpapers

Horizontal banner format for websites

Panoramic format for immersive storytelling

A scrolling vertical panorama

Circular format for logos or icons

Tiny thumbnail size

Postcard-sized format

Polaroid-style photo layout

Bookmark-sized tall and narrow format

Magazine cover format

Poster format with text space at the bottom

Oversized wide format for billboards

Full-page book illustration

Instagram carousel-style multiple-panel layout

Tri-fold brochure layout

Printed in Dunstable, United Kingdom